By the Book, ***FROM THE*** Book

From Humble Beginnings, to Tragedy, to Redemption

EDWARD L. ROMAN WITH JOHN DESIMONE

By the Book from The Book

Trilogy Christian Publishers

A Wholly Owned Subsidiary of Trinity Broadcasting Network

2442 Michelle Drive

Tustin, CA 92780

For information, address Trilogy Christian Publishing

Rights Department, 2442 Michelle Drive, Tustin, CA 92780.

For information about special discounts for bulk purchases, please contact Trilogy Christian Publishing.

Manufactured in the United States of America

10 9 8 7 6 5 4 3 2 1

Library of Congress Cataloging-in-Publication Data is available.

ISBN: 978-1-68556-346-2

ISBN: 978-1-68556-347-9

Dedication

This book is dedicated to my wonderful and beautiful wife. You are the lighthouse that continually brings my ship home, and I am forever grateful. I thank you for being a kind, loving, supporting, and forgiving life partner. You are a true example of Proverbs 31:10. The Virtuous Wife.

I Love you, and I always will.

Forward

Recently retiring as a Chief of Police after a thirty-five-year career in Law Enforcement, I often find myself reflecting on the many people I worked with, the challenges I faced, and the choices I made along that amazing journey. Maintaining a Christ-centered life while balancing family life with this demanding career is a daunting test of character and commitment. Along the way, I was privileged to work with this author, Edward Roman, who consistently demonstrated this remarkable character even in the most stressful situations, which inspired those around him, including myself. Just observing and being around Ed often caused me to reflect on my own actions while fostering a great deal of respect and admiration for this man who truly seemed to put everything in proper perspective while demonstrating his strong Christian character. As a fellow Law Enforcement brother, I would ask myself, "How does he do it?" and, more importantly, "How do I do it?"

This is an easy-to-read masterful work eloquently highlighting the importance of choices and priorities in life, especially as a Christian and a Law Enforcement Officer serving the public and in the nation's largest jail system while being a light for God in a dark place. Be prepared for a riveting journey with the author that will take you through dark valleys to mountain tops and every place in between. Whether you are contemplating a career in Law Enforcement or have served for many years, readers will get a front-row seat witnessing how Ed Roman and his family displayed their selfless love for those in need while navigating challenges, trials, tribulations, and victories. I wish I had read this book many years ago, as it would have undoubtedly had a positive impact on my life both personally and professionally. So, buckle up readers, you are in for a treat!

John Meyer
Retired OCSD Lieutenant - Chief of Police Services for the City of San Juan Capistrano, California

Retired Chief of Police - Irvine Valley College Police Department - Irvine, California

John DeSimone is a best-selling memoirist, editor, and novelist. He's co-authored bestselling *Broken Circle: A memoir of escaping Afghanistan* and others. He taught freshman writing at Biola University and has worked as a freelance editor and writer for twenty years. His current release, a historical novel, *The Road to Delano*, is a coming-of-age novel set during the Delano grape strike. He works with select individuals to chronicle their inspirational stories when not writing novels. He lives in Claremont, CA, and can be found online at **www.johndesimone.com**.

Table of Contents

Prologue
All Becomes Clear

I don't remember a time in my life when I thought of pursuing any other profession than becoming a sheriff's deputy. I knew nothing of the Bible, of God, of His calling, of His purpose until I was out of high school and a deputy in waiting. Even then, I had little clarity on why I should become a deputy other than a conviction of what path I should take in life. Does God direct those who don't know Him? Does God knit purpose and meaning into our beings from the very beginning of our existence? I didn't have answers to any of those questions until an event took place.

I had been an L.A. County Sheriff's deputy for six years when I transferred out of Men's Central Jail to train for a new position as a patrol officer. Within the first couple of weeks of reporting to the Norwalk Sheriff's station for training as a patrol officer, I learned my mother had fought her final battle with pancreatic cancer. My Training Officer received permission to stop by my family home to visit her one more time. We parked the cruiser in front of the house and went inside. My partner headed into the back yard patio to be with my family and I went down the hall to her bedroom.

She lay motionless in her bed, her skin drawn tight, and taking shallow breaths. I held her hand: clammy and calloused from a lifetime of work. It was only a matter of hours, maybe minutes, and she'd pass on to her final rest. Her eyes were closed, and I knew all sense and awareness of this world was fast fading. I was comforted in the moment, despite the sadness I felt at her passing. She had been a dedicated and hardworking wife and mother, raising all seven of us on my father's wages as a laborer. I was confident she would be with Jesus soon. I hadn't always had that assurance about her eternal state. Anger at my pops had consumed her later years—a good father but an unfaithful husband—until only a few months before when she made a decision that had ramifications for both of us. That event brought clarity, not only to her life but mine as well.

I wasn't always so certain about my mother's destiny after death; she harbored much bitterness toward my father because of his affairs. He had died the year before, and shortly before his death, he confessed and repented of his sins and received Jesus. About six months later, on a visit to my mother who was in bed struggling with pancreatic cancer, I remember telling her pops had accepted Christ and she said, "Hmmm, I wonder how he was acting up there."

Resentment rippled across her tired face. She turned her face away from me and didn't say anything, but I knew I had hit upon a hard knot of un-forgiveness as old memories flared up. She didn't want to hear good news about him, as if he had gotten away with a life of betraying her with his multiple affairs.

He had been a good father, a good provider, and had a strong influence on all of us for good, but he was an unfaithful husband. A truth that couldn't be denied. And in her last days, as she suffered from the pain of cancer eating away inside, old memories and resentments consumed her as well.

Busy with my new career as a sheriff's deputy, I kept in touch with her as much as possible. Then, about a month before she died, I checked in with her again. She was sitting on the couch in the living room. Everything had changed; her face was radiant, and her smile glowed.

"Ma, what happened?"

"Mijo, I forgave your father."

"Mom, that's great."

"Yes, Mijo, I forgave him. I talked to Dr. Lopez."

Dr. Lopez was a psychologist who worked in the neighborhood with youth and taught at a local junior college. A generous man, he had stopped by to see my brother Dave. He was positive and uplifting wherever he went, and whatever he had said to Mom had helped her through a difficult decision. The last time I saw her here hadn't felt like the right time to share the gospel with her because she was so angry. But now I explained to her how we were all sinners, and though what my father did was grievous, he had accepted the forgiveness of Christ. I urged her to remember that Christ had sacrificed for all of our sins, pops, mine, and hers. And that forgiveness and freedom from her bitter memories were hers for the asking.

"Will you pray with me, Ma, to receive Christ? Do you want to go to heaven?" She agreed, and she closed her eyes for prayer. There was a genuine earnestness in her prayer.

Then something strange took place, almost surreal.

Her eyes remained closed, and she began rocking back and forth. Was she having a seizure or some other medical emergency? Again, rocking back and forth, she kept it up with her eyes closed.

"What's wrong, Mom?" I thought to reach out and settle her when she opened her eyes and gazed at me.

"Now I know why."

"Know what?"

"Now I know why."

She pursed her lips and took a deep breath and exhaled. "Years ago, Mijo, I almost made a bad mistake. When I found out I was pregnant with you, I wanted to get an abortion. I was in my forties, I had a full-time job, and I thought I was finished having babies. I said, 'no more.'"

I could see this was a difficult moment for her, but she wanted to tell me. She said:

"I went to Tijuana, where your grandmother lived. She went with me to a house where I was about to have it done, you know. While we were sitting there, my mother turned to me and said, 'I don't think you should do this. This little boy is going to bring you a great blessing.' Her words went right into my heart, and I got up and left that house. I was that close, Mijo."

It was a sacred moment—in a flash, the significance of my entire life became clear. My grandmother had a prophetic moment, stating the boy in Mom's belly would be a blessing to her. There was no possible way she could have known there was a boy in Mom's belly. This was decades before pre-birth gender tests and ultrasound were available. My grandmother couldn't have known the baby was a boy—I was that boy.

"Now, I know why, Mijo, I didn't abort you."

My only reaction was to smile, and to myself, I praised God. He had knitted my being together in my mother's womb (Psalms 139:13). He knew me from the beginning of my existence and called me to be his child and serve my fellow man as a peace officer.

On the day she told me, I was thirty years old. Just a month later, on a June evening in 1997, my mother's eyes close for the last time on this earth, and I thanked God for great parents. Not perfect ones because I don't believe anyone gets those. But great ones who taught me so many important lessons that helped pave the way for my destiny.

That moment with my mother clarified why I was so focused on my future from my very first memories. It also explained so much about my fellow human beings. We are all knitted together tightly by God's grace in our mother's womb, and we're all granted by God's creative act a life to live. Some take it seriously, and some don't.

This story is about the miracle of life God gave me and how I lived it, what mistakes I made, and what lessons I learned, and how I became the man of God He wanted. And all the amazing and not so amazing people I met along the way.

Every day, as I submit to His will, God's purpose in my life becomes more evident and more powerful. So, in the reading of this book, I hope and pray you find your purpose for being, that you learn to grow by your mistakes, and live every day in the joy and strength of our mighty Creator. I pray and hope God's hand in your life is as clear as sunshine on the brightest days.

1

An Honorable Beginning

So many good things have come to me because of what I learned at home, from my older brothers and sisters who helped raise me, my mother who carried and fed me and made sure I had what I needed, but most of all from my father. He was never more than a laborer in his work, but in his family life, he was large. Yet, he carried himself with such dignity and integrity that he was known as Don Phillipe and my mother as Donna Vicky, honorifics seldom bestowed on those with callouses on their hands. In my estimation, he was made of iron, but he had feet of clay like all of us. But it was his iron will and deep wisdom that have made me the man I am today. It would be many years into my adulthood before I would read the commandment from the Old Testament, "Honor your father and mother (which is the first commandment with a promise) so that your days may be well with you, and that you may live long on the earth" (Gen. 20:12). He never spoke those words, quoted a book, or said this is what we had to do. It was a given, lived out because of our love and respect for our parents. My brothers and sisters and I lived by that truth in our home, and I have witnessed that its promise has never failed to be true.

My father, Juan Roman, was a man of great determination. When he found no opportunities for himself and his new wife, Victoria, in his native Mexico, he looked north. Following in the steps of so many to pursue a better life, he crossed into the U.S. in 1946. At the border, he presented his papers that read Phillipe Roman, a U.S.-born citizen. Phillipe was his younger brother, who had always lived in Mexico while born in the U.S. He was happy with his life and work in Mexico City, so he agreed to swap I.D.s with my father so he could pursue his dream. It was not a small favor my uncle had granted my father, but a once-in-a-lifetime opportunity to follow a dream of building a better life. At the El Paso port of entry, he had to convince the border guards he had not been in Mexico to avoid the draft, but he had lived in Mexico his entire life after his birth. Finally, the family was allowed to pass.

With the help of a family friend, the couple and two children, Victoria and John, settled in Selma, California, in a migrant commune for farmworkers. It was a rustic existence, with small cottages, shared bathrooms, and showers, but it was a start. My parents began picking grapes, following the migrant trail, and always returning to Selma. John, my oldest brother, started picking with my parents at five years old. After school, he went into the fields and worked side-by-side, doing as much as a child could do. Hard work was always part of my family's culture, a habit that became our heritage.

We moved to Los Angeles in the early fifties and settled in Rivera (later renamed Pico Rivera). My father moved away from the fields, and their seasonal tenuousness, to a regular job as a machine operator at Pacific Clay. He spent the rest of his career as a factory worker.

My parents intended to give us a better life and insisted my brothers and sisters attend school. We didn't have much, but our home was filled with love and respect for one another and, most of all, for our parents. My father wasn't arbitrary, wielding his power to have us grovel at his feet at every word. He didn't seek to control us as much as to encourage us—we lived in a land of opportunity. We needed to have our dreams and to take advantage of what America had to offer. He didn't want any of us to follow in his footsteps as a laborer. He made that clear to my brothers and me on several occasions.

Certain scenes are clear in my memory of his influence on me. After his shift at Pacific Clay, he would come home, and slump exhausted into his favorite chair. I used to kneel on the floor and help him remove his brick-flecked boots. In his exhausted voice, he said, "Mijo, don't be a laborer like me. Study hard…" He wasn't a man of many words. He didn't have to say much more. I understood his meaning. There is a better life ahead, but I would have to find it.

We lived in the projects, also known as the "campito"

or "little camp," for a few years until dissatisfaction set in. My sister Victoria, like my brother John, were popular in school and were bothered by where we lived in the projects. She was too ashamed to bring friends home and told my father that. This troubled my dad and one day after work, my father found his way to a real estate office in Los Nietos and spoke to Mr. Morris. He inquired about buying one of the new tract houses filling the new subdivisions. He had no down payment, so Mr. Morris lent him the down payment of $1,000 as a second for the down payment. The combined payment of $100 a month required Dad to take a second job, working as a gardener for one of the largest landowners in the area, Mr. Burk. He'd come home by 2 p.m., rest a bit, then take off around 4 p.m. for the orchards, to water, weed, and pick the fruit.

By the time I came along, the seventh child to a mother who was weary of childbearing, we had lived in the new house for a couple of years. My father was 52 and winding down his years of laboring, retiring in his early 60s from aching hands and knees that hobbled his body, but not his physical and moral presence in my life. My mother was 42, and I learned much later that another child forced her to consider taking radical action to terminate my life. Thankfully, she was talked out of it.

After I was born, she wrote to my brother John, who served in the Army in Europe, that he had a new baby brother. Unfortunately, he didn't believe her and wrote back that he thought she was covering for my sister Gloria. When he returned home, he even inspected my birth certificate.

Our home in Santa Fe Springs was four bedrooms, two bathrooms, and a tiny kitchen. A castle compared to the shack the family had crammed into in the projects. This was my home until I purchased one of my own with my wife when I was 25. It could be a rough area with the usual suburban ills that plagued poor neighborhoods—gangs, crime, drugs. Santa Fe Springs was a small industrial town of about 16,000 squeezed between Whittier and Downey. Too small to have a police force, the streets were patrolled by the L.A. County Sheriffs. When they rolled by in their black and white cars, kids and parents shrunk away. It was as if there was a corporate guilt everyone bought into, that because we were poor and Hispanic, we were all guilty by association, and sheriff's deputies threatened to find us out.

My father never bought into that way of thinking. I was about five when a car roared down our street and lost control at the bend in the road where our house sat. It jumped the curb and careened up onto the lawn of the house across the street from us. Sheriff's patrol cars pulled up, deputies went to work, checked on the driver, and took statements from witnesses for their reports.

I remember my father speaking respectfully to a deputy officer while the tall, well-dressed deputy in a khaki and green uniform took notes. My father's calm, respectful manner impressed me, and likewise, the deputy's respectful attention to my father. My father stood straight and proud. An honorable man had nothing to fear from those in authority. Why should he? He lived an honest life. None of his kids were in gangs. By that time, my older brother John had been in the army for four years and returned from Europe. My brother Daniel had received his draft papers to fight in Vietnam. We were solid citizens of the neighborhood. My brothers and sisters were busy with their careers and marriages and growing into responsible adults. My father had much to be proud of. No one in my family was afraid of the cops; there was respect, but no shrinking away.

A year later, I played in our front yard, and a sheriff's black and white cruised down our street. Most likely, I had spotted one before, but this day I wasn't distracted playing sports or running around, and so I waved at him, giving him a big smile.

He braked and called me over to his window. Standing on the curb, I could see into the cruiser. A blond-haired man in crisply ironed tan uniform with dark green pants flashed me a friendly smile. I asked him to blast his siren and lights. And he did. He then gave me a short tour of the car, pointing out the shotgun, his radio microphone, the switches for the lights, and the siren. I don't remember much of our conversation, but I knew he wasn't in the area to harass or bother us but to protect us. So, I had that immediate sense that I was safe talking to him. This man was out here doing good, trying to help, an honorable job. By the time he drove away, I was smiling inside and out. In my heart, I knew that was the job I wanted to do when I grew up. I wanted to be deputy sheriff, and wear that sharp-looking uniform, and do good for people. I couldn't have been more than six years old, but my mind was fixed.

And I never wavered from that conviction.

*

There are many ways children learn to respect and honor their parents. One that I experienced was watching how my brothers and sisters listened to my parents or didn't. When my brother John graduated from high school, he had a serious girlfriend, and he had a choice to make. Did he get married, or did he go into the military? The Vietnam war was just starting, and kids were soon to be drafted. He asked my father for his advice. My father counseled him to join up because he could serve his country. Counsel that would stay with him the rest of his life. John listened to his sage advice and found himself well situated both in the military and at the end of his hitch.

John had the hyper-responsible gene in the family. In the army, he refused to spend all his cash drinking and carousing. He observed that most of his buddies ran out of cash before payday and were out hustling loans from their friends. My entrepreneurial brother soon had a side gig lending out small amounts of cash at exorbitant rates. If someone borrowed $20, they had to repay him $40 on payday. He was so successful that he regularly sent my parents $100 a month to make their mortgage. This story became lore around our dinner table, and there were many others about my brothers and sisters taking care of each other.

My mother worked and made sure we had food on the table. Her frugality was legendary in our family. She had a way of stretching food to last, to live within her tight budget. John sending home the mortgage payment for several years was a sign of loyalty and respect for how hard my parents struggled to give us a better life. He understood the hardships and wanted to be a positive contributor. I don't think he ever verbalized that he was honoring our parents, but the meaning of his action spoke louder than words.

Our family gatherings were large and noisy. I grew up surrounded by nephews and nieces, celebrating the holidays as one large family: Easter, Thanksgiving, Christmas, birthdays, and other celebrations. While there was a lot of talking, swapping stories, music, dancing, and eating, there were never any open arguments or fights. On the contrary, our family always had mutual respect—my brothers and sisters enjoyed each other's company and didn't allow differences to bleed into the festivities. If there were differences, they handled them privately. As the youngest, I observed how to treat siblings, their spouses, and children, my blood relatives. We had a tight family, bound together by mutual respect and appreciation.

At our family gatherings, everyone showed up, with food and drink, except one—my brother Gilbert. Once he had decided to defy my father's advice, it changed the course of his life. In his senior year of high school, he got his girlfriend pregnant, a neighborhood scandal at the time. Dad counseled Gilbert that he didn't need to marry her. Young men were being drafted. My brother Daniel was in Pleiku, Vietnam, that year and would be home the following year. If Gilbert went into the army, he would learn a skill. But, instead, Gilbert chose to marry his pregnant girlfriend against my father's advice. This set a pattern for Gilbert's life. He decided to distance himself from the family. None of us were born black sheep, but Gilbert certainly wore that mantle throughout his life, deciding to go his own way. And we all watched the tragic circumstances that befell his family.

I had a unique perspective as the youngest because of my brothers and sisters and their respect for my parents. Working to support the family was part of growing up. My siblings worked at jobs they enjoyed and were good at, got married to spouses they loved and admired, bought their first homes, and had children. This was the pattern of a productive life I witnessed close up.

When I was eight, our next-door neighbor, Mr. Muela, asked me to help him out. I remember him asking if I'd cut his grass every week, and he would pay me. But, of course, I told him, "No."

A couple of days later, at dinner, my father gives me that look. I knew right off. I was in deep trouble. "Mr. Muela told me you didn't want to help him."

I was melting into my seat; heat flushed my cheeks. It was as if he was searing me with X-ray vision burning right through me.

"Don't ever do that again. Somebody asks you to

help—you do it. You help out around here—your brother John did it. Daniel and Dave too."

I didn't need any more prompting.

I knew that John started helping out when he was a five-year-old, doing stoop labor with my parents in the field. Then, as he got older, he worked and gave his paycheck to Mom, and she would make sure he got what he needed. Then, in his army days, he made enough to pay their mortgage. Dan, Dave, and my sister Gloria did the same thing, and I never heard any of them grumble or badmouth my parents. Life was a struggle to survive—that was the apparent reason for helping. But it was also a struggle against selfishness and meanness, against the tides of disrespect shattering families around us.

When I was ten, I had my first real job of delivering papers. So, what does a ten-year-old kid do with $20 a month? I gave it to my mother to help out with the house. I didn't do this grudgingly; I did it the way my older brothers had done it. My father was on permanent disability by that time, and $20 in the 1970s was enough for food for the week. I remember how proud I was to help out, handing her my pay. It was a lesson in selflessness as much as an economic necessity.

There wasn't a lot of hugging and kissing cheeks in our home. Instead, love was often more practical—a package of new underwear, a new shirt, or whatever we needed.

Mom always took care of us. That was a certainty I grew up with.

Looking back, I believe I learned in those episodes of giving that looking out for others is one of the greatest expressions of love and respect one can show.

My older sister, Gloria, was 15 years older and became a surrogate mother to me until I was in high school. I was a latch-key kid before it was a widespread problem. My parents were seldom home after school. So, I had to keep busy. I began playing basketball and baseball in junior high, and with school, sports, and friends, I kept busy.

My father's influence was never far. One day, a group of my friends was over, and we were messing around in my room. Dave and I were the only kids living at home, and I had a room to myself. My friends were goofing around, like kids do, calling each other by a derogatory name. After they left, my father asked me in Spanish what that word meant. I told him. He digested that for a second or two, then gave me that look again, the one that looked right through me. I knew what he meant. If my friends thought nothing of disrespecting each other using a derogatory term, what did they feel about themselves? Could I trust them? Why would I want them as friends?

It often didn't take more than a nod of approval or disapproval that influenced my siblings and relationships. He didn't have to tell me anything more. So, I backed off those kids and found new friends to hang around with.

*

My brother David, nine years older than me, wanted to join the California Highway Patrol. After high school, while he attended college, he sat for the Highway Patrol exam. For some reason, he didn't get hired. I didn't know why until I was about twelve when my brother Daniel took me aside. He knew of my ambition to become a policeman. He asked if I knew why David didn't get hired by the Highway Patrol, an ambition he'd expressed for many years. Then he told me the harsh truth—he had experimented with marijuana.

David had gotten as far as the oral exam, where he admitted to having once smoked marijuana. A regular question on all law enforcement oral and lie detector exams about an applicant's use of illegal drugs. In those days, that was an automatic disqualification.

I was blown away that something David had done as a kid, probably not thinking of the ramifications, had affected his future. I knew my brother didn't use drugs, but he had smoked it—once, twice, three times—it didn't matter. It could have been just a momentary lapse—had a friend passed him a joint at a party, and he took a drag—it was an automatic disqualifier.

Much to my brother's credit (something I admire him for to this day), he rebounded well. He continued his education—the only one of my siblings who went to a four-year university —and became a school administrator at Pioneer High School, his alma mater, where he had a great career. His presence during my four years at the school was instrumental in helping me stay on the right path.

With my brother's story lodged into my subconscious

and my dream of becoming a sheriff's deputy more vivid than ever, I entered Pioneer High School in 1981. If the '60s and

'70s were the hey-day of smoking weed and getting high, the '80s was the era of a drug pandemic more insidious than any before cocaine, easy to hide, and lethally addictive, swept through the neighborhoods like a plague of locusts. Kids were pushing cocaine in the halls, the bathrooms, in the gym, wherever. It was easier to get than a soda from the vending machine. In my mind, there could be no experimenting. It was a road I refused even to take a step down. It didn't matter what others thought of me; what mattered was if I could reach my goal. There were hurdles everywhere, and I intended to jump them. But unfortunately, many kids took the bait, and their lives were ruined before they even got started. Addiction is a tragedy: it stunts the intellectual, emotional, and spiritual health of its victims. I witnessed so many of my classmates wash away their potential because of early addiction. Witnessing the lethal effects of drugs on kids my age made me even more determined to reach my goal.

But girls—that was another matter. In my freshman year, I began hanging out with a senior girl. She was ready to graduate, and all her work was done. She wanted me to ditch a class with her, and I thought that was the coolest thing. I remember after we came back to school, walking down the hall like a big shot, I spotted my brother David storming toward me in the hall. How long had it taken for the teacher I had asked to be excused for the restroom to tell my brother I hadn't returned? Not long, I imagined. There was no reason to call my parents when my brother would handle matters. He stopped me in the hall and made it clear to me cutting class wasn't an option. I had to attend every class, every semester, or else. We never discussed "or else," but I imagined it had something to do with Dad.

It never happened again.

In my sophomore year, I made the varsity baseball team, and I never looked back. Baseball was my preoccupation. I wasn't much of a student, mostly C's; I involved myself in student government, something my brother Dave had done. High school was fun, if not academically rewarding, but I made my mark.

In my junior year, the travel team I pitched for made the Mickey Mantle World Series. It was a big to-do in our small town. After winning regionals, we were treated to an all-expense-paid trip to Tennessee to play in the World Series. We had a powerful and talented team, and I believed we had a great chance at winning all the marbles. But it wasn't to be.

We met Mickey Mantle, who sat at a table signing autographs while his beautiful wife stood nearby, soaking in the adulation of all the high school boys. It was an exhilarating moment to meet a legend to get to this point of achievement.

On the field, we won the first game. It was a double-elimination tournament, so we only had to win two out of three to clinch the championship. The night after the first big win, some of the kids on the team began to go crazy. It was a test of commitment for me. A teammate knocked on our door (three kids to room) and invited us to another room where they had some drugs or whatever. Another group of boys went to a local liquor store and stood out front, soliciting adults to buy beer.

I told them no thanks. I reminded them that the celebration should wait. They were jeopardizing the hard work we'd all put in to get here. They just blew me off. Finally, one of my roommates wisely agreed with me and stayed in the room. The other kid, a very talented ballplayer, let his dream go up in smoke. I don't if that was the start of his drug addiction, but his habit lasted long afterward, and from what I've heard in subsequent years, his life took a deep downward spiral into addiction.

I had so many cautionary tales in my memory, of my brother David, of my father's warning nods of approval, of witnessing my brothers move off into productive lives, that to throw my dreams into the wastebasket of stupid decisions didn't appeal to me. By no means was I a saint, I was just determined to make a different team, and I had a good idea what it took: a high school diploma and a clean record.

I graduated in 1985 without academic distinctions, but I graduated with a clean slate. And that, I believe, was an achievement I attributed to the values and support I received from my beautiful family—my dad, my brothers, sisters, and my patient mother.

The sheriff's department wasn't accepting applications from anyone under 21, so I had to keep busy and productive the next three years. And stay out of trouble.

2

Receiving The Savior

When I graduated from Pioneer High, my identity was set in stone. I was a "Roman," and I had a plan. I believe so many of the lost lives of young people stem from a lack of a solid identity, which points impetuous youths into the least productive but easiest to master occupations—crime and addiction. The love and discipline I experienced at home became the foundational stones in my character, but that didn't mean, as I would find out, I didn't lack for something more, something that would fill the deepest parts of my soul. My determination to honor my family's values served me well in high school, and once I graduated, I thought I had life by the tail. I knew what I was about and where I was going, but there was another plan for my life. One not written by me but written in heaven. "The mind of a person plans his way, But the LORD directs his steps" (Prov. 16.9, NASB). This is a truth I had yet to learn.

*

After graduation, all my friends from Pioneer went

right to work. We weren't college prep kids, so we expected to be in the workforce. Since I had at least three years before applying to the sheriff's department, I kept busy. My first jobs were ones I enjoyed but didn't offer much in career possibilities if the sheriff's department didn't work out.

I worked on the field crew at Whittier Narrows Golf Course. I had a blast shagging balls on the driving range, driving the little tractor that scooped up balls and blew them into a bin, while golfers pinged long drives off the wire mesh cage encasing the driver. I came to believe it was a bit of sport to see if they could hit me. I played a lot of golf, but it wasn't a sport that stuck with me.

At night, I attended classes at Rio Hondo Jr. College, trying to keep my study skills sharp. Truthfully, I wasn't a natural student, so I didn't pursue a degree. Instead, I began dating a nice girl, and we were falling in love. First love is such a euphoric experience; it certainly carried me away with thoughts of marriage and kids. As a sign of our seriousness, she convinced her father to hire me at his print shop and teach me a trade. I enjoyed that work, and I picked up quickly how to burn plates for the various print jobs. Unfortunately, she broke my heart.

After she dropped me like a bad habit, we were no longer a couple, I lost interest in the printing job since I would see her on occasion, and that was too rough for me. I worked for my brother John for a while at ITW Hi-Cone, where he'd moved up into a supervisory role. My last job was working for UPS at the Olympic hub. It was hard work, unloading and loading trucks, but I enjoyed the physical labor. I liked UPS and envisioned this job as a backup if my first option didn't work out.

I was taught to think that way—first a career that could sustain a family, then marriage, and then purchase a home.

My job was steady; my finances were stable, and I had purchased a new car—I was moving ahead toward my lifelong goal. Yet, as orderly as my life seemed, I was miserable inside. With no steady girlfriend to occupy my free time, I became overwhelmed with loneliness. It's hard to explain the sense of emptiness that came over me as soon as I left work each day. At home, in my room, the loneliness overwhelmed me. I didn't have one person in my life I could talk to, and it was hard to believe that anyone cared about me or what I was doing. I was 19, with few friends. I didn't drink or smoke, and my brothers and sisters were all married, having kids, living their own lives. My nieces and nephews were too small to hang out with.

At home, it was just me; my parents were old, and both were retired. My friends from high school were hanging out, but their gatherings were dominated by drinking, smoking pot, or doing coke. I didn't know if they were drinking and doing drugs because they were experiencing the same feelings I was. A desire to be one of them would be the only reason I would go to their drinking and smoking parties. But I had already made that decision—I didn't drink, and I didn't smoke or snort, so to them, I was an old-fashioned square peg in their cool and "with it" round hole.

When I was in elementary school, a neighborhood boy across the street had committed suicide. Only a sophomore, he had felt no one cared for him. That was the story that went around—he was a loner forced to confront the darkness of a cold world by himself. So, he took the only way out he could imagine. I couldn't relate to his problem then, but now I understood how he could arrive at that decision to end it all. The sense of being alone in the cold, uncaring universe drove me to thoughts of suicide—a way out of my loneliness, a way out of the feeling of not fitting into a world gone crazy. I could go drink and do drugs like my former high school friends. Drugs and alcohol would grease my friendships and anesthetize me, so I didn't need to feel the yawning darkness I felt inside, but it would cost me my dreams. Or I could stay home and sink into my misery. I felt unmoored in a world filled with confusing choices. Some days my head would spin trying to sort it out.

Unloading and loading trucks in the baking heat of Southern California summers kept me sane. It kept my mind off my inner crisis, but as soon as I left the depot, the dark malaise crept in. In those days, I plodded from one workday to the next, trying to keep my head above the depression that threatened to sink me.

In September of 1986, I attended a friend's birthday party where I met a girl with a great smile, Linda Romo. We hit it off, and I took her phone number. After that, we began dating and having fun. She brought some light and fun to my life, things I desperately needed. But when I wasn't with Linda, the loneliness crept in like a bad weather front, overwhelming me. I didn't want to live this way.

One Saturday night, I had a date with Linda (to go to party), but I was so depressed, I remember glancing out the living room window at the Suarez home across the street. The driveway was full of cars, and lights blazed in the windows. I knew David Suarez from grade school. His father was a pastor of an evangelical church, and David had invited me to attend a few services in the past. I had, but nothing stuck. They were friendly people, and I knew I could at least have a conversation with David. On a whim, I crossed the street and knocked on the door.

Who should answer the door but Benny Jacobo? He was married to David's only sister. I knew him from Pioneer baseball. A few years ahead of me, he was a natural talent, the star of the team. The then California Angels had even drafted him. One of the humblest and kindest men I've ever met, he stepped out onto the dimly lit porch.

"Eddie, what's going' on, man?"

I didn't say much; I just mumbled a few things. I was tortured inside, and Benny picked up my state with ease. He shared God's love with me, and I soaked it in. I'd never heard anyone speak of Jesus the way he did, a caring, loving Savior who had me in mind. He knew my weaknesses and strengths, my sins and pride, and

He accepted me. The only comparison in my mind to what Benny was telling me was my understanding of the Catholic religion. My mother was devout, and I often went with her to church as a sign of respect, but the ritual and the readings never touched that part of me that was crying out to God for something more.

That something was His Son, Jesus Christ. He had died for the sins of the world, for my sins, and wanted me to have peace and joy.

. Benny and I must have talked for an hour. Before we parted, he invited me to church at 9 a.m. the next morning.

"Yes, I will be there."

It was a chilly November night as I crossed the street. I sat in my car, thinking and then I broke down weeping. It's not something I'd ever done before, but my spirit was overwhelmed with both sadness and joy—I really can't explain my experience any better than that. God loved me, wanted to forgive my sins, and accept me as his child. A simple truth that profoundly changed my life. I don't know how long I sat there before I went into the house. I tried to sleep, but I couldn't because of more spontaneous weeping. Man, I could not believe how broken I was that night, and it all released in a flood of tears. All I kept on saying was "Lord, I'm sorry" over and over again. That night, my anguish and loneliness lifted.

I became a Christian on November 1, 1986, a landmark date in my life's journey.

Later that evening, I picked up Linda for a date, she

was all dolled up in a beautiful light blue party dress. We were supposed to go to a party that night, dance and have fun. But I had other plans. We sat in my car in a parking lot, and I told her about what had happened to me. She didn't say a word while I explained my conversion and my new joy.

After I finished, she told me she had grown up Christian but had moved away from her faith. She admitted she needed a conversion experience too and knew exactly what I was talking about.

That night I made a big decision that set the tone for our relationship—I had to stop seeing her so I could get myself squared away with God. She was shocked but accepted my decision. I didn't know what the future held for us—if we'd ever be together, but I had some work to do on myself and draw closer to the Lord.

The next morning, I met Benny and David at church and told them about what had happened. They prayed with me and my life from that moment changed. Thoughts of suicide were gone forever, replaced by a sense of peace and joy that I knew weren't from me but the Holy Spirit. I had to act on this new reality and rearrange some priorities in my life. I continued attending church with David, and soon I was part of the youth group, hanging out with other kids my age who were committed to Christ. In a matter of months, I was asked to join the youth group leadership and take responsibility for organizing Bible studies and events. Immersing myself in the Word of God brought an entirely new dimension to my understanding of God, his purpose, and his plan for my life. My new faith had transported me to a world of knowledge, love, and acceptance.

Two years passed, and out of the blue, I received a call from Linda on my birthday, April 20, 1988. We had seen each other only a few times during the time apart. She'd send me a letter, and I'd respond, but that was it. But on my birthday, I was pleased to hear her voice. She wanted to take me out to dinner. It was my sister's birthday the next day, the 21st, so we agreed to go to Steak and Stein. I had never stopped thinking of her, and as it turned out, she had never stopped thinking of me.

That night, I picked her up in my truck at 5 p.m. Wow! I was awestruck. She had on this navy-blue dress, and her hair was done up—she was gorgeous. But there was more to her than that. As soon as she was in the truck, I could tell she had changed inside too.

After a fun dinner, we sat in front of her house for hours talking. She had grown close to the Lord, and I had grown in my faith. We were both more mature in our faith, and in our understanding of what we wanted. That night, I knew Linda was the one. She later told me that she had loved me from the first time we'd met at the birthday party and had never given up on me. She also told me the two years we were apart she had a lot of guys asked her out, but she had turned them all down. We were both sure of what we wanted, and now we had the Lord working in our lives.

One year later, I proposed to her on my birthday, April

20, 1989, and married on November 24, 1989. We both lived with my parents to save our money to purchase our first home together. My parent's four-bedroom house was empty except for the four of us. Ironically, she worked at UPS too, at the Soto hub in Los Angeles, and I worked at the Olympic hub across town.

I counted the days to my 21st birthday, and I signed up to take the first step to join the sheriff's department—the written exam. To my disappointment, I failed the first attempt by one point. A 70 percent would pass, and I had a 69. Three months later, I repeated the test with the same result. Although I did fine on the multiple-choice section, it was the verbal section, a reading comprehension test, that I failed. So much of a deputy's duties entail writing and reading reports the reading comprehension part of the test carries a lot of weight. Some people in the know say it's better to be an English Major than to study criminal justice or any other subject before entering the academy. Everything you'll need to learn about the law, you'll learn in the academy.

Disappointed but not dissuaded, I sat for the Los Angeles Police Department entrance exam and passed the written test. I whizzed through the following sections, including the oral, but not the medical exam.

During my senior year in high school, I was under so much stress from my baseball coach, school, a girlfriend, and other issues, I'd developed a bleeding ulcer. I lost so much blood that I needed an emergency transfusion to regain my health. I healed, but it was part of my medical record. So, when it came to filling out the form that required my medical history, I listed my bleeding ulcer. Unbeknownst to me, that was grounds for immediate disqualification.

How had I not seen that coming? I was told I could appeal, and I did—twice. This was a tedious process of obtaining medical records from the hospital, doctors, etc. and submitting an appeal. I was denied both times.

So, I was back working at UPS, contemplating that this could be my career if I didn't make the force. Since the sheriff's department allows those who failed the written exam to retake it every three months, I signed up one more time. But what would I do when it came to filling out my medical records? Did I disclose my bleeding ulcer, which had only happened once, and never happened again?

At church, I spoke to one of the older men about my problem, and he reminded me of what Abraham did when he was in Egypt, telling Pharaoh that Sarah was his sister. We discussed why he would do that and compared it to whether I should report my bleeding ulcer. It was a one-time illness, and it had never happened again.

When the exam date arrived in July 1990, I was ready. I passed the test and decided not to report the bleeding ulcer, and I flew through the physical. But those two tests were only the beginning. I had been through the oral exam once before with the LAPD, and I was prepared mentally for the barrage of questions they would throw at me.

Next came the background check. This is an

exhaustive process where they want to weed out as many unacceptable applicants as they can. Because they had so many applicants, they looked for ways to disqualify as many as they could. The sheriff's investigator assigned to me, Dave Elsasser, took a hardline. He questioned how I could get through high school and not experiment with drugs, not even marijuana. I answered him squarely, "No, sir."

He shook his head incredulously. There was no telling how many times he'd heard that from an applicant only to discover the truth.

He kept pushing me; his skepticism seemed to rise every time I answered his question about drug use. I knew what he was doing, trying to turn me. They wouldn't have disqualified me if I had experimented with drugs as they once used to. Illegal drugs were rampant. But if I had experimented and I had lied about it, and then under pressure had told him the truth—that would disqualify me.

"No sir, I told you the truth. I knew one day we'd have this conversation, so I stayed clean."

Finally, he relented. "Okay, Roman, we'll see. You still have to get through poly."

That month they went methodically through my neighborhood and all my references, talking to ex-employers and my current one. Then, a few weeks or so later, I met with him again. He leaned forward in his chair, smiling at me for the first time. "You weren't kidding, were you, Roman. You never have done drugs and drink, have you?"

I just smiled.

I flew through the polygraph test as I had expected I would. That machine is good for what it does, but it can only truly single out the honest people trying to get away with not telling the truth. The practiced liars who show no emotions when telling a lie can get through a polygraph test, but it's still an important screening tool for law enforcement and is widely used.

Once I passed the poly and the psych evaluation, there wasn't much to do but wait.

On December 18, 1990, I received a phone call from the LA Sheriff's Department human resources.

"Mr. Edward Roman?"

"Yes," I held my breath.

"We'd like to make you an offer of employment as a Los Angeles Sheriff's deputy. Do you accept?"

Without any hesitation, "Yes, I do." My heart was beating so fast, I thought it would burst out of my chest.

The woman on the line gave me further instructions on what I needed to do next.

"Your class begins at the academy on January 4. Are you available to report?"

"Yes, ma'am!"

In less than three weeks, I would begin the first step to

fulfilling a lifelong dream. I had no illusions the academy would be a stiff test of my determination. I was ready.

The first person I told was Linda, who was as excited as I was. Then, during the holidays, with the house full of my family, I broke the news. There wasn't a lot of excitement or celebrating that day. I had talked about becoming a deputy so much getting accepted seemed anti-climactic.

That would all change in 18 weeks, on the day I graduated, but first, I had to get through the grueling rigors of the Sheriff's Academy. My life had changed in ways I had never planned. I was married to a beautiful and loving woman, I had become a Christian, and now I was ready to take the next step in my life—becoming a deputy sheriff.

3

My Dream Realized

On the crisp morning of January 4, 1991, I walked through the Los Angeles County Sheriff's Academy gates. I felt prepared for the next 18 weeks that would test every part of me—physically, psychologically, intellectually, and spiritually.

On the first day, everyone showed up in a suit and tie. There were 79 recruits in our class, and we all assembled for the first time in a classroom. The drill instructor assigned to our training unit said many things, but one statement set me back. He had each of us look at the man next to us, to the right and the left. They had arranged us in alphabetical order, so on one side was Rodriguez and the other Ruiz.

"Tomorrow, that person may not be sitting next to you."

Rodriguez looked at me, and I looked at him; then Ruiz gave me the once over, and I did the same to him. I knew in my heart I wouldn't be the one going home. If any of us had to go, it wouldn't be me. The course wasn't going to be easy, but I was prepared in my mind to do whatever it took, to put in whatever hours I needed to master the course the work and to pass the tests. The DI went on to explain we'd get two chances to pass a test with at least a 70 percent. Failing a second time was an automatic ticket out the door. Other tests would challenge us too—the physical training (PT), scenario-based training, weapons training, interpretation and application of the law, defensive tactics, driving skills, and report writing, which occupies a part of almost every day in uniform. The course's curriculum followed the State of California's Peace Officers Standards and Training (POST). Every academy in California uses the same curriculum, so training was standard across the state.

Part of the academy's experience is earning the right to represent the sheriff's department as a deputy. For the first four weeks, we came to work in suits and ties. We had to earn the right to wear the uniform one step at a time. That symbolized to me that it's an honor and a privilege to wear the uniform. After four weeks, we were allowed to wear the standard tan shirt and green pants without badges, emblems, or other markings. As we passed each stage of our training, we were allowed to add patches to our shirts. After firearms training, we were issued duty belts but with empty holsters. But we weren't given badges. That would be the final ceremony. Wearing the complete uniform represents a rite of passage, that we've passed the tests and have earned the right to become a deputy sheriff. That feeling of completion wouldn't come until the end of our training. I had a lot of work to do before that moment.

Many of the recruits had prior military experience, so the PT wasn't a surprise to them. But to me, calisthenics at 7 a.m. in 48-degree weather followed by a three-mile run was a shock; so was a drill instructor in my face, yelling out instructions and reprimands. I'd never experienced this before, but I quickly understood why it was vital to my success. Just like the military does in basic training, putting recruits under psychological stress breaks them down to build them up. The aim of the physical training—the running and PT, marching, and psychological pressure was a test of your ability to withstand situational stress. If cadets couldn't take the intimidation and tension here, how could they take it when they are on the streets facing gangs and violence?

Every class had attrition for various reason, but I would say the most common reason recruits quit—they decided the physical and emotional demands of being a sworn officer was too high. The training wasn't what they had expected. It's better they decided that now than getting in the jails or on the streets and not being emotionally and mentally prepared for dealing with the public.

The classroom work wasn't my strength. I had never considered myself a good student up to that time. But once I entered the academy, I adapted. My motivation kicked in, and I applied myself. This was what I had always wanted, and I was determined to excel in the material. There was so much to learn, codes, laws, rules of arrest, case law application, elements of a crime, traffic laws, and more. But I took good notes, and every night after dinner, I studied hard.

Self-defense training was primarily with the use of the baton. We used the PC-24, which is a 24-inch aluminum baton with a handle. I had never been in a fight before, so I had a lot to learn. They created scenarios we'd encounter on the streets, complete with yelling, shouting, and fighting, trying to be as realistic as possible. We learned how to search and cuff a person, and of course, weapons training.

I had never fired a gun, so I was in the group that had to learn from scratch how to use a weapon. We were trained on three weapons—the shotgun, sidearm, and baton. Tasers weren't a standard issue throughout the force until the early 2000s. Up to then, only sergeants had them. The sheriffs used Berretta 92F, 16 shots. They taught us every detail of the weapon. First safety, then how to break it down, clean, and assemble it—something I'd need to do regularly during my entire career. Then we had to be proficient with using it. Target practice at the sheriff's range was fun, and I was good at it. Shotgun training was fun too. I'd never fired one and learning the tactics as well as its operation engaged me.

The final weapons test was a timed obstacle course that started in the patrol car. Quickly transitioning to a standing position by the front fender, I had to fire the shotgun twice over the hood; then hit specific targets accurately with my sidearm. Again, I did very well on that test. We also learned driving skills, defensive tactics, and the skid-pan maneuver.

I looked forward to weapons training, as I'd given a lot of thought to the supposed conflict of a Christian carrying a weapon with good chances, I'd have to shoot another human. In conversations with the pastor of the first church I attended about my career choice, he was adamant a Christian shouldn't take a job that required a weapon. These conversations forced me to sort out my thinking on the difference between killing and murder. A killing can be accidental, self-defense, or in the case of war, national defense. Murder is opposite, and has malice and purpose to it, and is unjustified. After talking with a different pastor about my career, he helped me clarify the difference. I began to think of police work as a calling, a duty that I could perform to the glory of God, to protect citizens from the scourge of evil.

As a deputy, I would never have the power or right to murder someone, to take a person's life for personal reasons. That's against everything I believe as a follower of Christ. Instead, a deputy is an authorized representative of a local government, empowered to enforce the law, keep the public order, and protect the lives and property of citizens. Under the law's authority, I was charged to perform my job that included using lethal force only according to my training. So, I studied Romans 13 with care:

> *Every person is to be subject to the governing authorities. For there is no authority except from God, and those which exist are*

> *established by God...*
>
> *For rulers are not a cause of fear for good behavior, but for evil. Do you want to have no fear of authority? Do what is good, and you will have praise from the same; for it is a minister of God to you to for good. (Romans 13: 1 & 3,4 NASB)*

A sheriff's deputy's authority is a power granted by our Creator to organize and secure the safety of human societies. The authority and power are for the "good" of society. From my training in my home, I knew I was subject to the authority of my parents. As a sworn deputy, I would be under the authority of my superiors, with a responsibility to uphold the law. My job would grant me the power to use lethal force if the situation called for it. I had no reservations about doing my job.

I couldn't think of a more noble and challenging calling, putting my life on the line to serve others this way. For that reason, I had no problems with learning to handle and use weapons. I prayed regularly that I would never have to use them in a moment of crisis. But if I had to fire my gun, I asked God for wisdom and skill not to miss. I was prepared to take down someone who wanted to hurt others or a dangerous person who had to be stopped.

The world has many needs, and Christians shouldn't shrink back from working in legitimate fields. However, a person has to have a calling to do police work to remain sane. Going into police work with any other mindset than protecting and serving the public is a formula for disaster.

Not everyone is cut out to deal with all the things officers have to deal with every day. You have to have the ability to remain impartial and do your job. You can't break down under stress, and you must maintain a balanced temper and objectivity. This is a difficult attitude to maintain, but one that is instrumental to an officer's success. We deal with very evil people and maintaining your composure is important.

The correct temperament and tactics can diffuse so many volatile situations. Losing that delicate balance between objectivity and an even-temper can create situations that become permanent black marks on all who wear the uniform.

One day in early March, this was brought home to me when an event took place in LA that reverberated through police ranks across the country. During a class, one of the training sergeants rushed into the room. He was upset or excited about something, that much I could tell. He held up a VHS tape and waggled it at us. "This is what you don't do." With that, he turned to the video player, slid in the tape, and rolled it. The black and white images were shaky and dark, a scene lit by streetlights. But I could make out the shadowed figures next to the car with the driver's door open as if someone had just exited it. Men in dark uniforms surrounded a man who lay partially on the ground, attempting to rise, while four LAPD officers struck him with their batons using "power strokes." Rodney King became a household name after that night.

King had tried to evade a stop by the Highway

Patrol by speeding away, reaching 117 miles per hour. After exiting the freeway, LAPD officers had cornered him on a side street. He was drunk, high on drugs, and ignored commands to stay down on the ground. By the time a bystander had begun rolling his camcorder, King was half on the ground, looking up as if pleading for mercy, surrounded by officers reigning blows on him. The officers had struck King sixty times, breaking his leg, fracturing his jaw and wrist, and leaving him with multiple lacerations and bruises. His behavior justified his takedown, but not the brutality of his arrest. The officers' tactics would be questioned by every police and sheriff's department, every newspaper, and media outlet nationwide. The Rodney King arrest would go down as the poster child for the use of "excessive force" by police.

In the classroom that day, the sergeant reviewed the tape as a teachable moment. He critiqued their tactics—"If a man is on the ground, and the baton isn't working, use one of your other tools—leg hobbles, cuffs, a taser—don't keep doing what's not working."

I remember that day as if it was yesterday. It was a watershed moment in LA police history that forever marked the force as brutal and racist. After the publicity surrounding Rodney King, the public's attitude toward us changed noticeably. There are always groups who don't trust the police, but anger at anyone in uniform boiled to the surface after the tape of Rodney King became public. On our regular group exercises, we would run in formation around the streets of the academy. After the King incident, cars regularly sped by us as someone shouted out the window Rodney King's name, flip us the bird, or yelled some other angry epithet. People's anger at the police was palpable.

I didn't go into police work to beat and kill people, as some think of cops. Instead, I became a deputy to serve. That may seem naïve to some, who think cops are all about power and abuse, but I can say in hindsight, most officers I've worked with in my twenty-five years felt the same way. Did we have some bad apples, some abusers, some disturbed individuals get through the rigorous screening system I've described? Yes. Without a doubt, just as there are bad doctors, teachers, lawyers, bankers, and politicians. Police departments draw from the society around them and do their best to weed out the bad apples, but it's not always possible. I don't believe the LAPD officers involved in the King beating were bad apples—I fault their training, tactics, and leadership.

Those LAPD officers and sergeant Koons were charged assault and use of excessive force but were acquitted by a jury in superior court in Ventura County where the trial had been moved. The U.S. Department of Justice stepped in and after a grand jury indictment and trial, Sergeant Koons and Officer Laurence Powell were convicted of the use of excessive force and served thirty months in jail. The jury found that the last five of the sixty baton strikes constituted excessive force. If they had stopped when appropriate, their lives would be different.

The ramifications of the King arrests were astronomical

to L.A. with riots breaking out shortly after the Superior Court not-guilty verdict. The entire episode, the riots, the horrific aftermath of destruction to the poor communities of L.A. made a deep impression on me—good officers know when and how to restrain themselves and act appropriately.

A week before we graduated, the last ceremony took place. It's called the colors run. We run in formation, three miles up and three miles back. After that run, we were awarded the final insignia of our uniform, the most important one—our badge. Made of cloth, we were allowed to sew them on. It was a very proud moment for me, wearing the full uniform of a deputy sheriff. I had passed all the tests, and I had made the grade.

The graduation ceremony was the highlight of my time at the academy and my life. My entire family showed up. My 76-year-old father, my mother, all my brothers and sisters, and their spouses, and even some of my aunts and uncles from Mexico made the trip north to watch me graduate. Our class had lost ten cadets. Some decided early on the rigors weren't for them; a few couldn't pass the tests. So, 69 of us marched across the parade grounds that afternoon as the guests watched. We'd practiced our marching diligently, even coming in early to march in the parking lot to get it right. One of the cadets had been a Marine DI, and he took the initiative to teach us different cadences to help us polish our formations. That day in May, under a clear Southern California sky, we looked smart in our starched uniforms, with all our patches and badges, making our way across the parade grounds. I had dedicated all my spare time, arriving early, studying late into the evening, Saturdays and Sundays, and now I felt a swelling of pride to show off how hard I had worked the last four months.

We sat in the same alphabetical order as they called our names, and we rose, crossed the stage, and received our diplomas. After we had all done our walk, Sheriff Sherman Block asked us to stand, raise our right hands, and take the officer's oath.

"You rose up as cadets," Sheriff Block said, "and now, you will sit down sat down as peace officers of the State of California."

It was an emotional moment for me after dreaming about this since I was about six years old—seventeen years of waiting. I had often spoken of my dream, so when they heard of my acceptance into the academy, it didn't seem a good reason to celebrate. But that day in May, as my family gathered around me, with my wife and Sheriff Sherman Block in the frame, I believe the group photo captures how proud my family was to see me in uniform. Of course, all of them congratulated me as soon as the final shot was taken, but it was my 76-year-old father, the guiding force of our family, who came up to me, placed his hand on my shoulder, and whispered in my ear, for the first time in my life, "I am so proud of you, mijo."

I was still mijo, his son, the youngest of them all. But that day, I stood tall, a man among the men of my family. They had all grown as heads of their own families, carrying on the family legacy. Now it was my turn.

*

A few weeks later, on May 26, 1991, I reported a Men's Central Jail in downtown LA for my first assignment. All rookie deputies spend their first two years staffing the jails. County sheriffs are responsible for three main areas of local policing: the jails, the courts, and the transportation of inmates between city and county facilities and the courts. Sheriffs also patrol unincorporated areas of the county and cities that contract with them for patrol officers. But the jails are their primary duty and one that consumes many of the department's resources.

We had had some coursework and lectures on the jails. I had never been exposed to gangs and criminals—I hadn't run with that crowd. But the jails would be an education in what can go wrong in a person's life when their upbringing is stripped of honor and respect. So, one way I did feel prepared was spiritually. My reading of the Bible had given me a practical understanding and peace that I could strike a balance necessary in police work. God had shown me a verse, "When a man's ways are pleasing to the Lord, He causes even his enemies to make peace with him" (Prov. 16.7, NASB). So, I had a Spirit-inspired confidence that as I entered the jails, if I came to work each day knowing that I'm operating in the way of the Lord, I would do well and even bring some peace to some of those whom I served.

4

Men's Central Jail University

After high school, I went right to work for a golf course. It was fun, and I had a great time with my friends. But it was a job. I knew I would move on from it someday. But the day I reported for work at the Men's Central Jail on Bauchet Street in downtown L.A. was the day I realized my life-long dream. As gritty as jail work would get at times, I realized that this was my calling, not just my job. It would be a few more years before I discovered how God had intervened in my mother's life so that I was even alive to walk in those steel bars and doors in May 1991, but from day one, I knew this was where God wanted me.

After graduation from the Academy, I had spent an additional two weeks preparing for my jail duties. The training included tours of the jail for orientation purposes. Still, most of our training in jail operations took place at the Academy or at a firefighter training facility where we participated in hot-fire training. Because the jails were crowded and a fire would be potentially lethal to many of the inmates if deputies didn't have a plan, we were trained in basics fire-suppression skills by L.A. County firefighters. We learned to don turnout gear, boots, helmets, breathing apparatus, and basic skills in coordinated efforts to extinguish fires and evacuate inmates.

In late May, I was finally prepared to report for duty. We wore the cotton Class B uniform and carried the long heavy black flashlight and cuffs on a regular belt with no 9 mm Beretta or bulletproof vest. I'd had one tour with the Academy class, so I knew what the jail looked like. With the additional jail operations training, I also had an idea of what was expected of me. But no amount of training could prepare me for my first assignment. My duty station was in the High-Level module, where all the inmates were accused of Type One felonies—murder, carrying concealed weapons, assault, etc. These were bad dudes, and many of them were gang members and hardened criminals. I knew to be aware of inmates trying to get the best of the new guy. But I'd also determined that if I wanted to be respected, I had to respect everyone I spoke with—inmates, trustees, fellow officers, and civilian workers.

It was common for some of the older deputies, for whatever reason, to become condescending to the inmates, to not take them seriously, and talk down to them. Maybe they'd been in the jails too long. Dealing with the worst side of humanity day-after-day does grind on a person's attitude. If I let it, the work environment could grind me down too and destroy my conviction that these inmates needed to be respected as human beings. I was determined to treat everyone I met with the same respect that I expected in return. This was my mindset going into the jails. That is why I decided to prepare my mind every day for work from my first days on the job. On the drive into downtown, which usually took about a half hour, I listened to the preachers like Chuck Swindoll, who always had many things to say about one's attitude, and the grace God gives for the asking. So, I also had a prayer time, asking God to guide my thoughts and words and be his man in one of the toughest houses of detention in the country.

In my first days, I felt overwhelmed by the responsibilities, the sights, and the sounds. The physical plant itself presented a shock to the system. If you can imagine a stale gym locker times ten, that's about it. The odor of rotting teeth, or men who don't take showers. After a while, I didn't notice the odors of over 9,000 men packed into an aging jail. Men's Central is one of the oldest and most crowded county jails in the country. L.A. County in 1991 had the largest inmate population of any county in the nation, and it still does. In all the county facilities, there were on average 20,000 inmates. The equipment in the Central Jail facilities was outdated and was in constant need of repair.

On my first day, my training officer (T.O.), a tough veteran female deputy, showed me the ropes, handed me a set of keys, and said she'd be back to check on me as she had another trainee to supervise. She supervised me for the first month of my two-month training period. If I didn't meet expectations during that time, the training period would be extended.

The High-Level Unit, Module 3500, had over two hundred inmates, and I was one of two deputies tasked with overseeing them. Four rows of twenty-six cells with two inmates per cell. Two rows on one floor and two rows stacked above it on the second floor.

It didn't take me very long on the job to realize that I'd been granted a great deal of authority. I'm twenty-four years old, and I'm telling much older men what they can and can't do. I sensed early the awesome responsibility I had over all these human lives and wanted to be wise in the moment, but it wasn't always easy.

I performed hourly cell checks, shining my flashlight through the bars. Supervised "fish lines" of men who snaked through the unit, leaving, transferring to another facility or module. When a prisoner was transferred, I matched his JRC card with his name and handed it to the Deputy. There was a constant need to supervise fish lines leaving for and returning from chow time to inmate visits, church services, sick call, showers, and transfer lines. My head was spinning for the first few weeks.

Walking down the rows for security checks, inmates would crowd the bars and inundate me with requests, "Deputy, can I make a call," or "Hey, I need to go to the clinic." The requests were constant, so it was only natural for me to say "no" to many of them because of other demands. I was already supervising attorney visits, family visits, and a myriad of activities. There was no way I wanted to come across as arrogant, but you have to say no to just about every request but still have enough savvy and compassion to sort out the pressing needs versus seasoned criminals trying to play the system. The importance of listening and discerning came home to me early in my training.

Two inmate workers, Tommy and Jerome, called trustees, were worth their weight in gold to me. They were local street gang members who were in jail for robbery and murder. They were assigned to me on my first day, and they treated me with the utmost respect. They had earned the right to have more freedom and take responsibility. Inmate workers had special privileges in the housing area because, first, they were chosen by staff. Second, they had to have a certain credibility among the other inmates in the module. We would use them to clean common areas, pass out supplies, and handle any issues on the rows, cells, and court lines.

As a rookie, inmates would sometimes test me to see how far they could get one over on me. So, I understood that some, not all, were going to try to test the system.

Amidst a hectic day, an older gentleman came up to me and told me he needed to see a nurse. So, I thought, *Right, you need me to send you to see a nurse, but I know you want a clinic pass to go to other housing locations to meet up with other inmates.*

I told him, "No, go back to your cell!"

He looked a bit flush and had his hands over his heart, and it looked convincing for the most part. That said, I wasn't going to let this inmate get one over me, no way. As I'm speaking to him, Jerome comes up and says to him, "Hey, man, what's wrong with you?" The inmate tells him, "I got chest pains, and I need my Nitro." Jerome, with eyes wide open, as if he were having a heart attack, tells me, "Deputy, he takes nitroglycerin, which is a medication that people with heart conditions; you better get this guy to the clinic."

While at the Academy, we had a learning domain on illegal substances, no one had ever mentioned or identified common legal drugs and prescription medications inmates would legitimately need. For example, I had never heard of nitroglycerin as a medication. I knew it was used in dynamite, so I didn't see the wisdom in handing it out to inmates. Thankfully, Jerome was there. I saw the look on his face and realized I better get the inmate to the clinic. Jerome escorted him and returned about forty-five minutes later to the module and told me, "Whew, man, Deputy, that was close; he got worse and had a full-on heart attack in the clinic. Nurses called paramedics, and they took him to a hospital."

I think about that incident today and wonder, had I dismissed it and sent the inmate back to his cell, what if he would have had the heart attack there in his cell? Had I not allowed him to go to the clinic, I would have felt responsible. I would have to live with that, and I probably would have lost my job. Thank God for my inmate workers; I'll never forget those guys.

I had to learn and learn quickly to sort out the genuine needs from the fakers. Most of the men didn't even know the names of their medical conditions until they were behind bars and were given a medical evaluation when they were processed through the Inmate Reception Center. So, it became essential for me to know the symptoms of a heart attack or diabetic shock and what conditions needed immediate medical attention. The most common ailment, one easier to assess, was inmates complaining of shortness of breath, which were asthma symptoms. I would get them right down to the clinic for treatment with inhalers. Whatever they needed, bandages, meds, whatever, I never hesitated to hustle an inmate down the clinic.

My training officer regularly came to the module and pointed out different areas I could improve in, and she often helped out if I was overwhelmed. She would recommend areas I could improve in and noted what I was doing well. I asked her questions to clarify what I should do in certain situations, but I didn't want to appear weak or unable to figure things out independently. So, in the locker room after my shift, I regularly compared notes with the other deputies from my class. Nine of us had come over from the Academy. None of the graduates went directly to patrol duties, but the Central Jail wasn't the only posting. The C.J. was one of nine jail facilities spread throughout sprawling L.A. County. One man with a Class B license went directly to transportation since he had experience as a commercial truck driver. All of us envied him.

After a month, I was transferred to another module and began working with a different TO. Every day was another evaluation of some procedure or process until the jail routine became a habit. Another month of close supervision by an experienced deputy, and he signed off on training. I had completed training, and now I was on my own.

The goal each day was to learn all the different nuances of handling inmates, taking care of their needs, and keeping them alive. That wasn't always as easy as it seemed. Each evening, if the module had been calm, we could give the men what's called "freeway time." The cell doors were opened, and they could step out into the walkway we called the freeway. They could play chess, backgammon, or other board games, talk, read, or whatever. They were to stay in the module but watching all 200 or more inmates was a challenge. We were always on the lookout for "roamers," inmates who came in from another module, usually to cause trouble. One time, a roamer identified an inmate marked for a hit, entered the cell, and strangled him—then stuffed him under the bunk. His bunkmate feared for his own life if he ratted on the killer—no doubt he'd be next in line for the same fate. Silence is the law of the jail. We didn't find the dead body until the following day.

The time in the jail was an unmeasurable training tool. This was my first exposure to gangs, particularly the Bloods and Crips, the Mexican Mafia, and the many other gangs from all corners of the county. During my years at MCJ, I learned more about illegal and legal drugs I would encounter on the streets during my patrol years. In the jails, I witnessed the dark side of drug abuse and mental illness and the depths it sinks men into committing inhumane acts against themselves and others.

One night, I had to escort an inmate to the hospital after he ripped out his scrotum. He said the voices had prompted him, and it was the only way he could stop them in his head. On another occasion, two cell-mates fought over a Snickers Bar, and one of the men stabbed the other in the eye with a shank because he wouldn't give up his candy. As a result, that man lost his eye—over a candy bar.

Deputies are regularly moved around to give them exposure to all the units and different populations. One unit assignment opened my eyes to the power of the criminal underworld to survive and thrive even when behind bars. My time in module 1750 that housed the high-level gang leaders was one of those eye-opening experiences for me. Believe it or not, the Mexican Mafia rule inside the state and county jails. I wouldn't have believed it if I hadn't witnessed it myself. While during my tenure at Men's Central, I did not see any of the most egregious drug smuggling, which was exposed during the years I wasn't on duty there. I was told to keep my eyes open for their schemes. Whatever schemes they were running were too sophisticated for the average inmate to pull off.

The Mexican Mafia was born in the California prison

system to organize and control the lucrative market for smuggled drugs inside the system. They controlled most of the illicit drugs inside the entire jail system in California, in both state prisons and county lockups. They also controlled drugs sales in local neighborhoods around L.A. through exacting "taxes" on other gangs. If the local gangs don't pay up, they put out a contract. Crews usually pay up.

In the jails, the Mexican Mafia leaders are all doing long-term sentences. However, because their legal cases, appeals, or other legal maneuvers continue, they were at the Men's Central instead of being shipped off to state prisons. In addition, most of them had chosen to defend themselves under the "pro per" designation, which refers to a status where litigants defend themselves. Typically, maximum-security prisoners such as members of the Mexican Mafia have no contact with other inmates and few privileges—limited phone time, free time, and visitations.

That all changes when inmates claim "pro per" status. Under that designation, the prison authorities are legally obligated to grant them access to the law library two hours a day. Inside the law library, they have access to a bank of phones, which are unmonitored not to violate their client-lawyer confidentially. Pro per inmates are to use the phones to conduct legal business. They are also allowed to have runners, designated individuals of their choosing, usually wives or girlfriends, who delivered stacks of legal documents, law books, and other materials pertinent to their cases. Because of confidentiality restrictions, deputies could only glance through the materials but cannot read or closely inspect the materials.

These freedoms within the very restrictive jail environment made those who could play the system wealthy and powerful. The criminal minds have no limits to what measures they will go to exploit the weaknesses of others. The Mexican Mafia, a group of ruthless anti-social murders and crooks, took that exploitation to another level right under the watchful eyes of the L.A. County Sheriffs.

With its primary and most powerful leaders behind bars serving long sentences, they developed a way to control the drug trade inside the jails and outside in the neighborhoods typically controlled by local street gangs.

The Mafia members chose to represent themselves pro per. Most of them were already serving life or decades-long sentences for major felonies. With little to lose, they set up elaborate schemes to smuggle and distribute drugs inside. They chose runners who would do their bidding, often wives, girlfriends, willing visitors, or corrupt attorneys. The runners found ingenious ways to smuggle drugs into the jail. In his biography of the Mexican Mafia, Boxer Enriquez along with writer Chris Blatchford documents showed how one creative wife smuggled black tar heroin to her husband. She would iron black tar heroin into thin strips, peel back the flaps on large manila envelopes used to hold legal documents, and iron the drugs under the flaps.[1] Runners used hollowed-out law

---

1 Chris Blatchford. *The Black Hand: The Story of Rene "Boxer" Enriquez and His Life in the Mexican Mafia.* Harper, New York, 2008 pg. 116

books and thick stacks of legal documents. They would "keister" golf-ball-size bindles of heroin, cocaine, and meth wrapped inside balloons. Once past a search, they would go into the restroom, remove them, wash them, and pass them along to the inmate they were visiting. The inmates, in turn, would sell the drugs, distributing them to their network of dealers. This became the source of a lucrative drug-smuggling operation orchestrated by the most notorious killers and shot-callers in the jail system.

While I was at MCJ, we never caught any of the Mexican Mafia or their runners, except for an occasional bust of a girlfriend or visitor. But dealing with these maximum-security prisoners was an education in evil I will never forget. There is no better example of men who had completely given themselves over to lawlessness to perpetuate their crimes and exploitation. They placed themselves under the authority of evil and practiced it with all their energy.

5

Inmate Who Cried Daddy

It was the middle of June 1993 when my wife and I found out that we were to have our first baby boy, and we were so excited. I figured with a growing family; I would pick up some extra overtime shifts. Working O.T. was a common occurrence in the jails. Our department was short-staffed. At times we were using up to 2,000 hours of overtime a week, which was crazy. And I tried to be a part of it. On this particular day of O.T., I was assigned to work on module 2700, the Crips module. The cells were designed for two men each, but we usually had a floor sleeper or two. It was a busy housing location that consisted of high-security inmates who were not choir boys. My shift ended at 2200 hours, so at about 2100, deputies would conduct a wristband count. I would go down every row in modules A, B, C, and D and check every inmate's wristband, which had each one's full name and booking number. An inmate worker would walk the row with me carrying tablets holding Jail Record Cards (JRC's). After finishing the count, I would match who was still at court and account for the missing inmates. At 2130 hours, the last of the inmates returned from court, and since all inmates were accounted for, I was clear. It was now time to relax and wait for the next shift to make relief.

The last inmate returned from court and headed back to his cell. He stopped and asked me if he had received any mail. He was a big guy, an African American man, who stood about 6 foot 4 and probably weighed 280 pounds. I gave him his mail, and I asked how his court day went. He said today was his sentencing, and the Judge gave him twenty-five years in State Prison. What surprised me is how he casually said it, "Twenty-five years in the Penn." It was like saying, "I have to go see a doctor" or "I have to go to the dentist," which expressed a slight concern but no big deal. Incredible! "Twenty-five years for what?"

I asked him, and he told me that his sister's boyfriend beat, sexually assaulted her, and put her in the hospital. He became so angry he found the guy and beat him so badly he ended up dying. So, he was found guilty of Second-Degree Murder.

I thought to myself, "What a tragedy," and I told him I would keep him in my prayers. His whole demeanor changed as his eyes began to water, and he became somber when I said that. This big mountain of a man's story tumbled out of him--his dad left home when he was seven years old and pretty much abandoned him. He said he was very close to his dad, but his mom was always angry, and they did not get along. Finally, his dad was so tired of all the tension he left the family, never returning.

I remember his words that I will never forget, "Deputy, I know that if my Daddy had been in my life, things would be different. I wouldn't be here." He said this with tears and heartfelt emptiness and pain; I had to maintain my composure.

At this time, the early morning deputies started arriving for the next shift. Again, I wished this inmate well and again told him I would be praying for him. Years later, I began to read a book called Disciplines of a Godly Man when I came across this passage:

Men, as fathers, you have such power! You will have this terrible power till you die, like or not in your attitude toward authority, in your attitude toward women, in your regard for God and the Church. What terrifying responsibilities! This is truly the power of death. For this reason, we live in a time of great social crisis. Whole segments of our society are bereft of male leadership. At the other end of the scale, some strong men give their best leadership to the marketplace but utterly fail at home. We are men! And if God's purpose does not happen with the sons of the Church, it will not happen. Men, there are few places where sanctified sweat will show more significant dividends than fathering. If you are willing to work at it, you can be a good father. If you are willing to sweat, you will see abundant blessings.

*Do not be critical

*Do not be overly strict

*Do not be irritable

*Do not be inconsistent

*Do not show favoritism

God has created our children with their hearts turned toward ours. Our power is awesome; we must take God's Word to heart.[2]

The unfortunate truth about the story of the man who cried for his father is that it wasn't isolated. Most all the men I met and talked to had come from fatherless homes. It was well known among the Sheriff's staff and the law enforcement community that fatherlessness contributed to the criminal behavior of both men and women. Like the just sentenced man, so many young men suffer from anger over their abandonment. But most don't understand the root cause of their anger and take it out on authority figures—teachers, mothers, employers, and most noticeably, the police. Kids suffering from abandonment suffer a lack of self-control and severe identity issues. This explains why so many young people gravitate toward gangs whose leaders become surrogate parents, teaching them how to survive in a world that doesn't care whether they live or die.

---

2 R. Kent Hughes, Disciplines of the Godly Man. Crossway Publishers. July 2019.

I am reminded of a comment a Commander with the LAPD made in a lecture I attended. He said that, "I believe I have an answer to crime in our society. When mothers and fathers start becoming good parents, we'll see crime stop—because it starts in the home. When you affirm your children and love and discipline them, you equip them to go outside the home. Then they know 'I have the love, the security; I have everything I need to come against evil in the schools.'"[3]

I have also found much wisdom in James Dobson's radio show and writings. One of his statements on parenting has stayed with me, "The greatest gift you can give the world is a well-disciplined child. They will make good students, employees, and employers…"[4]

If there is one common factor in the men, I met during my first six years in MCJ, it's a fact they were almost all fatherless. While it's true nationally that fatherless men commit about 60 percent of all felonies. But that's across all ethnicities and socio-economic groups. In the MCJ, most felony convicts come from the poorest and most crime-ridden neighborhoods in Los Angeles. In my estimation, about 90 percent of the men I met and dealt with and were housed in MCJ were fatherless. There are too many studies to cite on the topic, but a few stand out. A Heritage Foundation investigation reported that,

over the past thirty years, the rise in violent crime parallels the rise in families abandoned by fathers. That

---

3 Author's Name Unknown. LAPD Commander speaking at parent-teacher event.

4 James Dobson. Radio Show

high-crime neighborhoods are characterized by high concentrations of families abandoned by fathers. State-by-state analysis by Heritage scholars indicates that a 10 percent increase in the percentage of children living in single-parent homes typically leads to a 17 percent increase in juvenile crime. The rate of violent teenage crime corresponds with the number of families abandoned by fathers.[5]

A growing number of children, black, white, and Hispanic, are growing up with absentee fathers. The ramifications for children in single-parent homes are staggering. Children in father-absent homes are four times more likely to be poor. In 2011, 12 percent of children in married-couple homes lived in poverty, compared to 44 percent in mother-only families.[6] Children who have no strong parent bond early tend to end up gravitating to violence. "Children born to single mothers show higher levels of aggressive behavior than children born to married mothers."[7] Often this childhood aggressiveness causes kids to gravitate to others, and in the impoverished sections of our cities, those are the established gangs. Gang life has its own culture of respect and lines of authority that are anti-social and violent.

These are the kids we see as adults—angry, volatile, with hair triggers for violent action, but at times, when

5 Fagan, Patrick. 1996. The Real Root Causes of Violent Crime: The Breakdown of Marriage, Family, and Community. Crime and Justice, Washington D.C. : Heritage Foundation.

6 U.S. Census Bureau. "Children's Living Arrangements and Characteristics." March 2011. Table C8. Washington D.C. 2011.

7 Soborne, C., Mclanahan, S.(2007) "Partnership Instability and Child Well-Being." Journal of Marriage and Family, 69. 1065-1083

they drop the gang persona, they are deeply human.

Fatherlessness contributes to drug addiction, aberrant childhood influences such as gang and criminal activity, and a host of social ills. So much of the evil we see in the jail resulted from fatherless homes that exposed young men and women to influences they neither understand nor could control. The spiritual oppression I witnessed in the jails and outright demonism is never recognized for what it is. Instead, these aberrant behaviors are classified as mental illnesses. Many cases are genuine mental illnesses, a chemical and physical imbalance of some sort, but not all. The worst cases have a deeper cause. I believe that God exists, and likewise, there is a real devil known as Satan. Maybe you doubt my words and think this is a religious myth or a fable no one believes in anymore. All I can say is all you have to do is work in any of the county jails for a while, and you'll become convinced otherwise.

What brought this fact home to me was when I met Erik Menendez, one of the brothers convicted of brutally killing their parents. I was working overtime on the graveyard shift in unit 7100, a medical unit of individual cells. But because of the size and privacy of the cells, high-profile inmates are also assigned these cells. They're the size of a small bedroom with a bed, a sink, a toilet, and solid doors. I was doing my hourly checks of the cells when I looked in the small, barred opening. Erik Menendez said, "Deputy."

His voice sounded troubled, so I opened the door, and he sat up in bed.

"Sir, you got to get me out of this cell. The room gets cold, I hear voices, and something ripped the pictures off my wall."

I turned on the light. The Menendez brothers received a high volume of mail, mostly from women who included with their letter's photos; many of them were provocatively posed. Erik had used toothpaste to attach them to the wall in a large collage. Now the wall was one big smear of white. All the photos were in a crumple on the floor.

"Come on, man; you did that!" I said. Just as the words left my mouth, I felt a horrible sense of evil come over me like a dark shadow. Then I remembered who lived in this cell for years.

"You know who was in this cell for the longest time?" I said.

"Exactly, sir. You've got to get me out of here."

The serial killer and kidnapper dubbed the Night Stalker, Richard Ramirez, had been in this cell for nearly five years while on trial for fourteen murders, often scratching pentagrams on the victim's walls. He terrorized the Los Angeles and San Francisco area for months, sneaking into open windows or doors, kidnapping children and molesting them, or shooting and raping the adults until he was captured by an enraged mob in East Los Angeles. He openly practiced Satanism, praising Satan in the courtroom, and spent hours calling down Satan, chanting like an animal in this same cell. He etched a pentagram on his palm and the wall—the same wall Erik had covered up with the photos. There are still stories in the jail of frightened deputies and nurses by Ramirez's dealings with the devil.

Sadly, there was nothing I could do for him. "Erik, we're full. I can't move you."

These demons are often territorial; once called upon, they stay in the same area. Not long after this episode with Erik Menendez, I was again on a graveyard shift, which I regularly worked for many of the six years I was in the Central Jail. One night, one of our three-deputy team needed rest. We often relieved each other during the quiet morning hours when the inmates were asleep, and we only needed to perform cell checks. Again, I was working the 7100 unit, and the Deputy went to the doctor's office to use the bed for a few hours of shut-eye. After an hour, he returned and looked as white as a sheet. We tried to get out of him what had happened, but he was too shaken to say anything. The next shift we worked together, I asked him what had happened. He explained that he was lying on the bed when the room suddenly grew cold, so he was shivering. Then a dark cloud passed through one wall and hovered over him. He was so frightened he couldn't speak or move. It finally passed through the far wall, and the room returned to normal. The incident so shook him, and he couldn't talk when he returned to the module.

Though there are dark influences within the jail, God is not without a witness. I was determined to let the light of Christ shine whenever the opportunity arose. Deputies on the graveyard shift are assigned to supervise the trustee work crews that clean the mess halls. These are usually low-ranking offenders serving less than a year for contempt of court, drug possession, drunk driving, etc. For two weeks, it was my turn to supervise a crew of two dozen inmates. We'd start around 10 p.m. and finish around 1 or 2 a.m. After their work was completed, their pay was to eat a meal served to the deputies, which was more delicious than inmate food. So, after they got their chow, they sat down together. But I wouldn't let them eat until we had prayed for food. The first night, I could see them glancing around, eyeing each other like, "Is this guy for real?"

But after a while, I could feel the tension released from the room. I knew God had shown up, and I sense His presence. After a few nights of praying, I then asked them for any prayer requests. After a few moments of hesitancy, one by one, they spoke up, asking for prayer for girlfriends, wives, kids, mothers, grandmothers, and their court dates—the stuff of life they cared about. So, I prayed for every single one of them. I prayed for their mothers, their children, their court dates—everything that concerned them. Toward the end of our time together, I began asking them for praise reports—what's God doing in their lives. Several spoke up:

"Man, I'm so grateful; I only got time served."

I'm thinking, okay, cool.

"Yeah, you know what, my wife called me, and she's doing good and the kids...."

I could see the other men lifted, glimmers of hope in

their eyes. God used me to bring the presence of God into their lives—light instead of darkness.

Before their time with me was finished, I asked one night, "Anyone here want to know our Lord and Savior, Jesus Christ." A couple of guys raised their hands, and I prayed for them. A few received Christ, and I'm grateful for the opportunity to be a witness to the light of Christ.

I never failed to admonish the men—I reminded them that the only reason they're in jail was because of selfish behavior. There was no other reason. They didn't put their loved ones first by taking care of whatever business they needed to. Instead, they got themselves into trouble doing their drugs or drinking, or whatever had separated them from their families. Most all the men were fathers, and they had shirked their responsibility to their families. I encouraged them to put their loved ones first when they're tempted to do something selfish. I knew they listened.

A week or so after my shift with the cleanup crew, I supervised a chow line when an inmate came up behind me. He said, "Excuse me, Deputy."

I turned to him, "What's up?"

"I don't see any wings on your back."

"What do you mean?"

"Those guys you worked with last week, they think you're an angel from God."

I smiled, "Oh yeah?" Those men were talking about the Deputy who prayed for them. I hoped when they left here, they remembered those moments we had together and took action to be better men. I praised God for the opportunity.

As soon as I broke through their hard shell of "I'm in jail," I noticed that it's easy to recognize they are humans like everyone else. Almost all the men had kids, wives, girlfriends—a life beyond their current situation. It's difficult, but possible, not to define them by their incarceration—they weren't all hardened criminals. But they all had made selfish choices.

I did my best to find ways to relate to them as humans during my six years working in the jail. One successful way was with music. Before lights out at 2200 hours, I would send the jail workers down the rows to tell them if they kept the noise down, kept out of fights, and had no other disturbances, Deputy Roman would play some music for them. In the little room that served as my observation station, I had a clock radio and a microphone used to make announcements to the entire module. If all were quiet and well-behaved, just before lights out, I would rubber band the button on the mic to keep it open, place it by the radio speaker, and tune it to an oldies station in L.A. called Kearth 101. They played music from the '60s & '70s, Motown, some rock, that kind of stuff. A sense of peace came over the module. I could hear men singing with the music—it didn't matter their background or gang or ethnicity—music had the power to reach down to the common core of their humanity—who didn't need love, respect, a sense of belonging, meaning, purpose, family. For a few moments before shut-eye, they were reminded there was more to their lives than spending time behind bars. I imagined it gave them a bit of hope for something more. I prayed that it did.

6

The Real Training Day

Norwalk, 1997. Halloween night. I'm on patrol learning the ropes, riding shotgun with my T.O. at the wheel. A call comes in and I'm working the MDT (Mobile Digital Terminal) and a 211-armed robbery in progress at the Wienerschnitzel on Imperial. Four suspects in white sheets. Four ghosts. Perfect for Halloween, a nightmare for us. My T.O. wheels the car around, lights and sirens on, and we roll.

"Four suspects southbound on Woods Ave. on foot." My T.O. orders a containment. Deputies who arrived at the location radioed that a passerby reported the four suspects fled on foot and entered an apartment complex next to us. We pull up to the two-story building, possibly an old motel with interior halls and apartment doors on each side. Apartment Units were on each floor, with a large laundry room in the middle.

I thought we had lost them, and I figured they were gone. They could be anywhere. That wasn't what my TO thought; a sharp cat, he said, "Okay, they got to be in one of these apartments."

We searched a floor at a time, apartment by apartment, carefully and quietly walking the long halls, listening for noises, scuffles, any clue to where they went. Finally, at the center of the complex, we entered the laundry room. My partner pulled out of the trash four bedsheets with eye holes cut in them.

He nodded at me. "They've got to be around here somewhere."

As soon as he said that we heard a door open, we both looked in that direction, and four black males stepped out. One of them was counting a large wad of bills.

With guns drawn, we both shouted, "Get your hands up. Get your hands up." They all complied slowly. My heartbeat was so fast it felt ready to burst.

The mother of one of the kids shouted at us from the doorway. She yelled, "Hey, they didn't do nothing."

Yeah, I'm thinking. We got the money. We got the sheets. Now we have to find the weapon.

We put them up against the wall and frisked them. I found the gun in a front pocket. I got the weapon and cuffed him.

We got the money, the gun, the disguises--everything we need to make the arrests—a textbook case. Later I realized it was a B.B. gun. But that didn't change the seriousness of the crime.

By not stopping at the front doors, thinking they had

disappeared, and we'd never find them, we persevered in our investigation, recovered the stolen goods, and solved a crime. At this point, I'd only been on patrol duties for four months and was still under the supervision of a training officer. He was an excellent street cop who took great pride in doing a thorough job on every call. That night he taught me how not to give up and use investigative techniques to solve crimes. I had so much to learn about being a good cop. Protecting the public is a solemn duty all the officers I worked with every day took seriously.

*

I had spent six years working in Men's Central Jail, four years longer than typical. But because of budget cuts and staff reductions, I couldn't transfer out. But my time had come to move on to patrol duties. I had never been part of the street life that typified gang member's experience. I didn't have any friends who were hardened criminals like many of the prisoners I met. Instead, my life had been intentional; I knew what I wanted and where I wanted to go, and that early decision made later decisions so much easier as I grew older. I'm thankful to my parents and siblings, who showed me the way. So, during my six years working in the Men's Central Jail, I learned all about crime and criminality; I considered it a crash course in lawlessness and poor decision-making.

Interestingly, every deputy gets the same powerful crash course, but they don't all react to it the same way. Some became jaded and tended to carry the angry edge into their professional and personal life. Then the daily stress of working with men constantly on the edge of sanity and society seeped into some deputy's marriages and relationships.

It became apparent the stress could kill me, or the constant exposure to evil could destroy my humanity, and I would become jaded, sour, and pessimistic toward work and life. Neither of these alternatives was acceptable to me. Through the power of Christ in my life, I prayed God would keep my heart open and human. It's the wisdom of His Spirit that I learned to separate who I am from what I did. At the end of my shift, my uniform went into my duffel, and I stowed my badge and equipment, and I became Ed Roman, father, husband, brother, and friend. I refused to let this job bury me. I refused to be the policeman of my family and neighborhood and bark orders like a drill sergeant.

While six years at MCJ was a long time, I enjoyed my tenure. The hours were predictable, and there was copious overtime. With a set schedule, I became involved in my children's lives. My father had provided a perfect home where I learned the meaning of authority, self-discipline, and the value of hard work. As significant as those values have been to my life, my father never attended one of my baseball games, never took me to a ballgame, and otherwise was too busy to have much involvement in my life. If it weren't for my siblings, I would have been entirely alone as a youth. He dispensed his wisdom but not his time. It just wasn't something he did. I know my father did the best he knew how. But I missed that father's touch in my life, and I had determined I would operate differently. I had seen a different model. At church, I witnessed how the Godly fathers participated in every aspect of parenting. They were involved, and their families thrived. They set the tone of a godly home with discipline, love, and nurturing. Then I observed fathers who weren't involved and the repercussions for their kids. It wasn't hard for me to see what I needed to do.

Working in the jails allowed me to establish routines with Linda and, by now, two young boys. My usual shift, from 10 p.m. to 6 a.m., allowed me to be home when she worked. She still held a day job at UPS, and she kept working until we purchased our house in Whittier. Unless I worked overtime, I kept to those hours, five days a week. We attended church together; I coached their baseball and football teams, getting to know the other parents and their kids. When the Angels played home games, the boys and I could get there early, watch batting practice, and get in a few innings before we'd go home so I could shower up and dress for work. My brother John often took vacations with his children, even flying them to Hawaii. So, we went on vacations together, ate meals, and prayed together as a family. It was everything I imagined a family could be.

I built a different life for us than I grew up with, and I felt good about it. But my time in jail had to come to an end. I chose not to extend, and truthfully, I was ready for a change. So, before I transferred to patrol duties, I prepared my wife that our life would be different. I would be working more hours. When I was required to show up in court, I might work 18 to 20 hours straight. Plus, as the rookie in patrol, I would be working weekends. Our new weekends would be Monday and Tuesday. All that said, I looked forward to the change.

On June 1, I reported to the Norwalk substation to begin my training as a patrol officer.

Patrol is the most common career path for deputies. After the initial two-year posting, deputies can apply to transfer to any open position they qualify for. Patrol work opens up so many opportunities for promotion and enhancement in the department. It also introduced me to the different world of policing. In the jails, men came in who had been arrested and booked. But how did that happen? They had committed a crime or were accused of such and were arrested and booked. I'd learned the legal and procedural side of working the streets in the academy, but nothing can replace on-the-job training. I learned firsthand the entire investigative process, the everyday diligent police work that makes so much difference to a safe community. And, of course, the paperwork that accompanies every interaction with the public has to be done correctly and accurately. After every arrest, a police report is required, and a Probable Cause Declaration (PCD that is essential to give you legal standing in an arrest.

The laws are clear that all citizens have fourth amendment rights against illegal searches and seizures.

My second T.O. was a professional dedicated to the craft of excellent police work. So, I was privileged to have a true professional as my guide to what a good cop could accomplish on the mean streets of L.A. And they can be mean to the innocent and unprotected.

Working the streets takes time and preparation. I arrived one hour before my shift and began to process of getting up to speed. I dressed, checked out a shotgun and ammunition, a bean bag, vest, and other equipment. Then I loaded up my assigned vehicle and attended a briefing before rolling out of the station at 2200.

On the first day, with my second T.O. sitting in the vehicle, ready to roll, he gave me a speech I will never forget, one I took to heart. He told me that officer safety comes first. "We go home to our families after every shift." He emphasized the importance of taking precautions of following procedures. So much of police work appears routine, but traffic stops are far from routine. You don't know where a driver is coming from; it could be a robbery, could be a murder. You don't know what's in the trunk. Hands kill cops, so always ask to see their hands. He continually impressed on me the need for officer safety.

*

Work wasn't all tension and adrenaline. Policing is about relating to people, and one of the most unpredictable parts of a deputy's life is how one responds to the daily encounters with people—in other words—temptation. Officers are human, and the forces at work in society, drug abuse, alcoholism, infidelity, greed, arrogance, and abuse in its many forms, are at work in deputies' lives as well. It's a constant battle, and I can attest to the reality that I struggled with temptation, and I believe God saved me from so many potentially compromising situations.

One that stands out to me was when I received a call of a 415E (loud disturbance party) in the city. I acknowledged the call, and I went enroute. It's a Saturday night during late spring, and many celebrations are going on during June. I arrived on the scene, and I could hear dance music coming from the residence's backyard. Obviously, a celebration was in full progress. As I got ready to knock on the door, a slender and attractive woman opened it. She appeared to have had a few drinks. She said, "The music's too loud, huh?"

"Are you the owner of the residence?"

"I just graduated from nursing school, and we're having a little party."

"Congratulations! Can I speak to the owner?" I'm trying to be as polite as possible. This was a harmless crowd, and they just needed to lower the volume.

Another attractive female came to the door. "This is my house."

I identified myself and told her I wasn't opposed to celebrations. But unfortunately, the music was too loud, and neighbors were calling the station and complaining. She apologized and said she would have the music turned down.

Just as she apologized, the first female came outside and stood on the porch, and asked me, "What time do you get off of work?"

Not only was I surprised by this question. I had just got off patrol training, and I had never come across this situation before.

"My shift ends very late." I thought that would cut off any further conversation. But it didn't.

"I'm going to be here all night." She gave me a charming smile.

There was a definite gleam of desire in her eyes that made my heart beat faster. The thoughts I was entertaining at that moment were against everything I believed as a man of God. A married man of God, at that. I was shocked at myself that I was entertaining thoughts that were completely contradictory to my faith. I kindly thanked her for the flattery and told her I couldn't come back.

She smiled and said, "Okay, but I'll still be here if you change your mind."

In retrospect, I should have done what Joseph did when being tempted by Potiphar's wife. Run! (Genesis 39:12). Trying to avoid temptation is not enough. I should have emphatically stated, "No!" Then moved on to the next call for service. As I walked back to my patrol car, she continually stared and smiled in a very seductive manner, and unfortunately, that visual lingered.

It's a busy Saturday night, and I'm going from call to call, engaging in what we call "Doing the Lord's work," keeping the streets safe. Periodically, throughout the night, the image of that attractive woman with a pleasant smile flashed through my mind. As my shift was about to end, I finished my reports and headed back to the station.

It's decision time. Am I going back to that party?

I'll just go for a few minutes, I said to myself. I can handle this. It's just meeting some friendly people; no harm in meeting new friends, right?

Continuing northbound toward the station because I'm off-duty in twenty minutes, a call comes over the radio: "Attention all units, eta's Code-3, 273.5 now. Children can be heard in the background crying. Unit in one or less? Code-3," lights and sirens. (A 275.5 is a California Penal Code section for Corporal Injury to Spouse.) The address of this crime is an apartment complex well-known for drugs and gang activity. So, I knew exactly where this drama was taking place, and I was about a minute out.

I acknowledged and told dispatch I could be at the location in one minute or less. I was immediately given authorization to roll, Code-3 (Authorized emergency response). Nothing gets the adrenaline flowing as much as rolling on the scene with lights and sirens. All of the training kicks in, and you're ready for any situation. As I arrived with another unit, my partner and I found the apartment. We see a man standing outside breathing hard, and we hear children crying inside. Other deputies started arriving at the location, and it turned out the husband was drunk and decided to assault his wife because she would not have intercourse with him.

After sorting out all this chaos, I asked the field sergeant, "Who has the handle on this call"?

He said, "King-2, (call sign). Who's King-2?"

"I'm King-2!" I said, surprised.

"You have the handle."

"I'm supposed to be off already, and there are units just starting their shift, with trainees!" I thought to myself, This should not be my call.

After getting witness and victim statements, I head back patrol station with one in custody sitting behind me. I get to the jail, and after booking and finishing all my paperwork, it's already three hours later. The watch sergeant told me to put in a slip, which meant I would get some overtime. As I walked out of the station in the early morning hours, it hit me. I was so busy and focused on my job, I forgot about what I wanted to do—go to the nurse's graduation party. I got to my truck, put my gear in the back, and I sat there and reflected.

I am thoroughly convinced God intervened that night. You might call it a coincidence or unlucky, but it was the protection of the Holy Spirit, keeping this fool from making a big mistake. I got that 273.5 call because I was not supposed to be flirting with that temptation, acting contrary to my beliefs. I love the way R. Kent Hughes put it in his book, Disciplines of a Godly Man:

> *Men, if we are Christians, it is imperative that we live pure, godly lives in the midst of our Corinthian pornotopian culture. We must live above the horrifying statistics, or the church will become increasingly irrelevant and powerless, and our children will leave it. The church can have no power apart from*

> *purity. This demands that we live out Paul's dictum: "Train yourself to be godly." --- holy sweat.*[8]

I can't say I know what could have happened if I had gone back to that celebration and met that woman. But I doubt if anything good would come out of it. In the end, God protected my walk, my character, my relationship with him, and possibly my life.

*

During my two years in patrol duties, I learned something new every day. All the theories of the academy became a daily practice. Every incident required a report. If, at the end of an arduous eight-hour shift, I still had reports to fill out, I did it on my own time. If I made an arrest that night, I had to book them, interview them, and fill out the report along with a PCD. Each interview and report could take a half-hour. An eight-hour day easily could turn into ten or more. In those days, I didn't get paid overtime as I had in the jails because I worked in a contract city, which meant minimal overtime.

On days I had to show up in court, I often had just enough time to go home, shower, change into a new uniform, and return. It wasn't worth going home at times because courts opened at 8:00 a.m., and I was off at 6 a.m. I took a nap in the station, then headed over. If I had time between cases, I could get some shut eye in the attorney's lounge. Someone would call me when it was my turn.

8 R. Kent Hughes, Disciplines of the Godly Man. Crossway Publishers. July 2019.

There were some very long days. So, I worked more and made less, but as arduous as the job was, I enjoyed it. There is a satisfaction in doing good police work that is hard to be understood by an outsider. Police are often characterized by their mistakes, the bad apples, and the extreme incidents of racist behavior. But day in and day out, thousands of my comrades put their lives on the line to make the streets safer and do an excellent job.

During my time at Norwalk station, one of the most gratifying incidents involved a tour bus full of Japanese tourists. There must have been a couple of dozen tourists in a bus returning from Disneyland. These were the late '90s, the days of expensive 35 mm cameras, video camcorders, and all of that electronic gear coming out of Japan. Their bus had turned into the hotel's parking lot, drove through the Porte Cochere and into the back of the lot to let them off. Before any of them could move, three thugs jumped on and robbed every single one of them. They put guns in their faces and demanded everything. They took every valuable: cameras, wallets, purses, watches, Disney goods, rings, earrings, anything shiny and valuable looking. Then they skedaddled.

We get the call—a 211, an armed robbery. I'm still in training, so it's not my handle. The handling unit called in— "It's a J.O. now (just occurred). The suspects were last seen heading northbound on the five freeway. Three black males." The handling unit asked assisting units to check the area of the 5 and the 605.

"Can I have some more units on the 91?"

With the senior deputy's experience and savvy, he figured they would be headed northbound back to L.A. And then down to Long Beach or Compton. A deputy spotted the car northbound on the 5 Freeway, so now we notify the CHP. The robbers exited the 91 freeway in North Long Beach. They're traced to a trailer park where they dumped the car. Officers call a canine unit, and the dogs sniff out the three hiding under one of the trailers. It was a successful operation that exhibited the best of teamwork by dedicated professionals.

I'm in training, so my place is to assist. I took one of the males and placed him in my vehicle back to the station, where I booked him and completed the paperwork. The handling unit stayed on location and obtained victim statements, what was stolen from whom—watch, camera, Disney apparel, etc. Today all of this information is typed into a computer form, but back then, each officer kept a notebook with all the information, and then back at the station, filled out the report by hand. Another officer on the scene found all the loot in the abandoned vehicle and returned it to the station, where we laid it out on tables in the briefing room. Every item is photographed and cataloged. It took total teamwork of all the deputies to track the criminals, catch them, and return all the loot to the station. No one got hurt, and every item was recovered. All of the training and expertise of so many deputies kicked in to respond and perform, acting quickly to corral the bad guys.

The most gratifying moment occurred when all

these terrified Japanese tourists, who spoke little if any English, filed in and stood along the wall. They gazed in appreciation at all their belongings laid out on tables in front of them. Not one item was missing. Then, they began to cry, bowing and thanking us in the way they knew how—by showing us respect for our efforts. I was very grateful to have played a small part in such an outstandingly successful operation.

The men and women I worked with, not only that night but for my entire career, were dedicated to the craft of keeping the bad guys off the streets and protecting the community. I witnessed their success in many ways, large and small; I can't tell every story. But suffice it to say, it's unfortunate that what's reported far and wide in the media are the screw-ups. Indeed, they should be, but there's no balance in the media with the everyday actions of deputies stepping into harm's way to make our neighborhoods safe.

After two years on the streets, and I was ready to move on to a new assignment. As much as I enjoyed the challenge of patrol duties, the irregular schedule had caused upheaval at home. Linda and I discussed what would be the best for our family, and I thought it would be better to return to an assignment like the jails where I could have a more predictable life.

So, at the two-year mark, my transfer request went through. I thought I would be returning to the MCJ, but another door opened for me.

7

Becoming Foster Parents

Every year, new assignments opened up in different departments. As much as I enjoyed the challenges of patrol, the hours put my family under increased stress. The Norwalk patrol assignment offered little paid over time, despite constantly working, because of the department's contract with the city. It wasn't unusual for me to work a 12-to-14-hour shift and get paid for 8. My understanding is this situation is no longer the case in city contracts, thankfully. In late 1999, an assignment at Los Angeles County Medical Center (L.A.C.M.C.) opened in the jail ward, and I jumped at it.

The Jail Ward took up the entire 13th floor of the rambling L.A. County Hospital, and I was assigned to maintain the security and safety of inmates and medical staff. Law enforcement agencies throughout L.A. County brought suspects and inmates to the facility who needed treatment for any injuries, sicknesses, and diseases. Any condition the county jail could not treat, the person ended up on the 13th floor. We had doctors, nurses, and other professional medical staff on the floor, which was an extension of the hospital, along with an entire staff of sworn deputies. It's a jail and a hospital, and the patients are still inmates, looking for ways to feed their addictions.

During one of my shifts on the jail ward, a nurse came up to me and said while she was dispensing medication to inmates, one of them stole a syringe off her medical cart. These carts carried all the medications, bandages, ointments, syringes, and other medical supplies nurses dispensed to inmates during their shift. I asked the nurse if she knew who it was, and she knew exactly who it was. I thought to myself, Why would an inmate need a syringe? He probably had drugs since it's easy for inmates to get them: methamphetamines, heroin, cocaine, marijuana, whatever is on the street is in the jails. On a daily average, there are 19,000 inmates in the L.A County jail system and many of them use and sell narcotics while they are on the streets. It's a large and lucrative business, both on the street and in the jails.

The nurse escorted us into the ward and pointed out the cell where the suspected inmate had a syringe. It was a single-person cell with a hard metal door. Four of us quietly positioned ourselves outside the inmate's cell. We counted to three, and at "go," my partner abruptly opened the door catching the inmate by complete surprise. In a beautifully executed textbook raid, the syringe lay in plain view on his bunk. We had crashed his jail party.

We took him out of the cell and searched it. We found contraband but no drugs. When we asked him where he had hidden his stash, he said, "I don't know what you're talking about."

"Really, you don't know what we're talking about?"

We conducted a more thorough search, and we came up with nothing. We strip-searched him, thinking he had keistered it. (The practice of hiding drugs in balloons and inserting them into their rectum.) Still no drugs. We grabbed hold of his right arm and exerted some pressure, and after a bit of persuasion, he finally told us.

"All right, all right, all right, I'll show you where it's at."

He opened his mouth, reached in, and pulled out three tiny balloons containing a dark substance. Incredibly, he had them hidden in the gaping cavities in his teeth. I had never heard of that, let alone even seen it. It blew me away—three tiny balloons of Tar Heroin. We took them into evidence and charged him with possession of narcotics in jail. He was placed on "Discipline," which means he didn't receive visits or phone calls.

People will often tell me that starting a career in law enforcement working the jails is a waste of time. Or, "How can you work with a bunch of criminals where it stinks and is dangerous?" To that, I say, working in a jail is an immeasurable education. Working with the criminal element daily trains a deputy to be street-savvy and instilled a greater awareness of officer safety.

Everything I learned in the jails I used while patrolling the streets. For example, when I came across suspected drug users, I would body search for weapons or contraband and then tell them to open their mouths.

Lessons in the jails weren't only about their criminal activity and how to outsmart them. But I also learned about the subtle movement of the hand of God and His infinite care for ones the world wants to forget and write off.

On another night shift, it was about 2 a.m., and I was conducting a security check on the ward. I entered a room with six inmates who were all on gurneys and were asleep. I was about to exit the room, and I noticed one inmate was awake. I acknowledged him with a nod, and as I walked away, I heard the Holy Spirit tell me, "Talk to him."

I stopped, and I said to myself, "Lord, I don't want to talk to him."

Again, I heard, "Talk to him."

Reluctantly, I said, "Okay." I asked the inmate his name, which I learned was Ronald.

"How're you doing?"

"Not good, deputy."

"What's wrong?"

"Docs gave me about two weeks to live."

I couldn't help but notice he was very thin and sickly looking. A sudden and deep sense of compassion come over me. I thought to myself, "This man is dying. Does he know Jesus?"

"Ronnie, if something happened and you were to die, would you go to Heaven?"

He looked at me with a puzzling stare and said, "Yes… no…I don't know."

"Would you like to know for sure?"

He smiled and answered, "Yes."

I inquired if he wanted to accept Jesus as Lord and Savior into his heart. I asked him this question based on Romans 10:9, "If you declare with your mouth, 'Jesus is Lord,' and believe in your heart that God raised him from the dead, you will be saved."

I told Ronnie, "We're going to pray, repeat after me," and as we prayed, it seemed like we were the only people on earth at the time. After we prayed, and he received Christ as his savior, I congratulated him on his decision and told him that I'd see him in Heaven one day.

"Thank you, deputy," he said with a weak smile.

"Take care, and sleep well." I went on with my security check. At the end of my Friday night shift, I went home for a three-day weekend. I came back to work and wanted to check on Ronald to see how he was doing. He wasn't in the room anymore, so I asked the attending nurse where Ronald went. I figured they had sent him back to the county jail, or maybe he got an early release. She glanced over the inmate receiving, and discharge book, then looked at me and said, "Ronald died two days ago."

At first, I was shocked and a bit sad, but then I thought, "Lord, you are incredible and merciful. In Ronald's last days, you loved him enough to allow him an opportunity to spend eternity in Heaven."

I thanked the Lord for the opportunity to be used for His kingdom. I hadn't given much thought to this episode until many years later when my pastor asked me to lead a team of twenty-five church members on a mission trip to Nicaragua. Initially, I didn't want to go on this trip, let alone lead a group. I then realized that I was making this all about me staying in my comfort zone. But the Holy Spirit spoke to me and said, "Go."

Immediately, I remembered Ronald in the Jail Ward on that incredible night I witnessed God move in someone's life. I decided to lead that team of missionaries to Nicaragua, and God used us to represent his glorious name to the children and people of that country. Being obedient to the Lord is a must for a Christian.

The book of God in Deuteronomy 5:33 states: "Walk in obedience to all that the Lord your God has commanded you, so that you may live and prosper and prolong your days in the land that you will possess."

That's a solemn promise of God that is as true today as it was in the days of Moses.

*

Besides getting almost every weekend off, I worked copious overtime during the week. The increased income brought significant changes to our little family.

With two little boys at home, Linda needed to stop working full-time out of the home. So, with my pay increase, she quit her job at UPS, and we were able to purchase a larger home in Whittier, one with a pool and more bedrooms. As much as we enjoyed the pool and more room, this wasn't for our enjoyment alone, as it worked out.

That year, Linda and I felt led that God wanted us to become foster parents. It is hard to work daily with the bleak ramifications of broken homes, fatherless homes, parentless homes, and worse still, abusive and irresponsible parents. So much criminal activity could be prevented if fathers stayed involved in the kids' lives, they conceived. On top of the epidemic of fatherlessness, the poor and minority neighborhoods of South Los Angeles were deeply traumatized by the cocaine, and then the crack cocaine epidemic that swept through their communities, wiping out entire families in some cases. Drug-addicted parents become the worst parents, offering little in the way of direction and discipline that children are desperate for.

The motivation to become foster parents didn't come out of the blue. Yes, Linda had a cousin who had foster children in her home, so we did have some exposure to how rewarding it could be. For myself, I remember from my days back in patrol the previous year dealing with parents who abused their children. The predicaments and dangers that moms and dads put their children in impressed on me how valuable stable homes with two parents are in raising children. But some incidents stood out and were pivotal in God opening my heart to commit to foster kids from difficult situations. We had no idea who God would use us as foster parents and what profound changes he would bring to our family.

*

In mid-October, my T.O. and I responded to a call from a nurse at Downey Community Hospital, who reported a case of possible child cruelty. While Downey was out of our patrol area, the parents and child involved lived in Norwalk. Officer Mejia and I met with a nurse who had treated an eight-month-old Stevie, who had arrived in full cardiac arrest. She had observed suspicious circumstances surrounding his injuries that were not consistent with the mother's story of what had happened to the child. The nurse had observed bruising around the neck, bruising on both cheeks, under the right eye, and chin. None of these injuries were consistent with the mother's story.

In speaking with the doctor who treated little Stevie, he concurred with the nurse's story and stated the child was in a life-threatening condition and was about to be transferred to Long Beach Memorial. The doctor said the injuries appeared to result from severe abuse, beating, strangulation, or both. Before the child was transferred, I documented the injuries with photographs. My T.O. was meticulous in investigating the events, and I took copious notes as he queried the mother and her live-in-boyfriend. He claimed that when putting Stevie to bed, he was coughing. So, he gave him some cough syrup, and that's when he stopped breathing. Then, he gave him CPR while the boy's mother called 911. The bruising and other injuries resulted from his efforts to revive Stevie. The mother's story was even less likely, but she claimed she didn't see anything as she was in the other room while her boyfriend gave the child the cough medicine.

My T.O. and I went back and forth from the doctor to the boyfriend, to the mother. Their stories didn't match up with the medical staff's assessment that the child had been abused. The child couldn't have received the injuries from CPR alone.

I used my notes to compile a meticulous seven-page report at the station, one of the more detailed reports I'd ever done. We then reported the incident to the Department of Children Services, who followed up with the mother and child at Long Beach Memorial.

A few months later, I was called as a witness to appear in court. Little Stevie had died before he even reached his first birthday. I was met in court by the detective handling the case. She thanked me for writing such a detailed report. The detectives used the thorough interrogation by T.O., Deputy Mejia, and my careful documentation to successfully prosecute the boyfriend for second-degree murder. He was convicted and sentenced to twenty-five years to life in prison. It didn't seem possible for the story to get any sadder, but the trial brought out that Stevie was the child of her previous boyfriend, who had abused her during their relationship. So, they took it out on little Stevie, and the boyfriend got twenty-five to life for his evil, but she walked.

The evil happening to children on the streets and twenty-five to life in the homes of my city is heartbreaking. Unfortunately, physical injury is not the only kind of abuse—neglect comes in many forms. Once, we rolled up to an apartment in response to a concerned neighbor's call of possible cruelty to children: children between the ages of 3 and 10 years old left alone.

Going into situations like this, we never know what we will encounter. The home could be orderly, but more often than not, the children are hungry, underfed, and in dirty clothes. But in our wildest imagination, we could never foresee what we found.

After knocking, a neighbor ran out of an apartment next door and said she cared for the children. But she wasn't in the apartment with them. Inside, we found the three kids—10, 8, & 3 on the living room floor, asleep. The room stank with the stench of urine, cat feces were smeared on the wall, and the carpet was stained. A filthy cat litter box lay next to the sleeping children's heads. The apartment was not only messy but filled with the stench of animals. Checking the rooms, we discovered that the kids were asleep in the living room. The back bedrooms were filled with cages of animals. We took the children into custody and turned them over to Child Protective Services. Then Animal Control removed all the animals. Their count listed ten cats, four rats, thirteen mice, one snake, two dogs, one ferret, two guinea pigs, and twelve rabbits.

We were called later in the evening to return to the apartment by the angry mother. When she returned home and found her animals and children gone, she was livid and called, thinking we would return them. But, instead, we arrested her for willful cruelty to children.

Once I had to arrest an intoxicated mother after she beat her thirteen-year-old son. When I responded to a 911 call, I found her son bleeding and bruised and her nine-year-old daughter crying. I found the mother next door drinking with a neighbor. When I confronted her, she was not only disrespectful but admitted to beating her son. There was also a one-month-old baby in her apartment. The mother was too drunk to take care of her children, and we arrested her for child abuse. Upon handcuffing her, the mother looked her daughter and said, "See what you did." The little girl was the one that called 911 and because of this guilt she became distraught and stated she wanted to commit suicide while crying hysterically. After the paramedics treated the boy and left, and relatives showed up to take the children, I remember sitting in my vehicle, my heart broken for these kids and so many others I had witnessed in my short time on patrol. I asked God what I could do to help kids in these situations, even if it was just a little thing. That's when fostering kids began to become an option for my wife and me. It's the little bit we can do to help kids in distress.

I knew that the Social Services Department in L.A. County was flooded with new wards. They actively recruited foster parents, responsible adults who could take these kids under their wings and give them a chance. Usually, assignments weren't permanent but were opportunities for the parents or guardians to get their life situation turned around so the kids could return to their homes.

We signed up through an agency called Olive Crest that acts as a clearing house for parents and individuals who want to foster children. The entire process took a few months for us to get through—fingerprinting, background checks, an interview—but eventually, we were approved and told we'd get a call when the need arose. And the needs were constant.

Our first placements were two siblings, a boy, and a girl. After that, Linda told me she didn't want to foster toddlers. Both of our kids were small, and she couldn't take more small children. We decided that we wanted to work with teens. I don't know why we thought bringing teens into our home with two small impressionable kids would be a good idea, but we had peace in what God wanted. If we were to be judged on the number alone of kids that came and went, some rather quickly, we probably wouldn't grade out as the most successful foster parents.

When we received a teen into our home, we always ensured they were comfortable and had what they needed—clothes, food, school material, visits to the doctor, dentist, etc. We treated them as we treated our children. We had a bedtime, a mealtime, and expectations of attending school, doing homework—all the things expected of me as a child. We opened up all the opportunities to them that were available to kids their age. Some kids were in our home for a brief period. One principle behind fostering is that the home offers a temporary place of stability until the kids are reunited with their parents. Often this took place, but only as the result of supervised parental visits, where the kids are gradually introduced back into the home. Meanwhile, the parents are working with Social Services to rectify the problems that caused the kids to be taken away in the first place.

Linda became intimately involved in this process with any of the children who came into our home. She kept a full schedule of parent meetings, social service visits, doctors, dentists, schoolwork, etc. Whatever it took to get the child on a path to success, Linda oversaw it as long as they were in our home. Mostly the kids adapted, and many of them returned home with their parents, which is the best outcome. But a few didn't like being told when to go to bed, take a shower, or sit down and eat with the family. So, if they weren't reunited with their folks in a short time frame, they usually ran away.

We learned first-hand how challenging it was to establish respect for authority in the child who came from a home where the chain of authority and respect had been destroyed. Much of the work deputies did in the jails was enforcing limits on men who had no sense of self-discipline. Most of them learned this way of living at home. As for the teens from Olive Crest, they did bring a level of stress into our family. But we weren't deterred. God did not want us to give up. That much we were confident.

Despite the disappointments, Linda and I were still open to welcoming more kids into our home. But we were wary. What dysfunction would the next child bring into our home? So, the next time, I would ask more questions about the kid's situation, making sure it was a good fit. Then, one day, a social worker who knew us from Olive Crest called with desperation in her voice.

"Ed, we need a good home. Is yours available?"

"What's the situation?"

"A 15-year-old-female. Can you take her?"

"How bad is her situation?"

"Ed, she was assaulted by her mother and siblings. She has some bruises and a cut." It turned out that there was a significant altercation in the home, and officers were called. They decided they couldn't leave her in the house.

"Has that been taken care of?"

"Yes. Everything's fine. We just need a home for her."

She had just turned fifteen, and it sounded like she might make a good fit for us. From the desperation in the social worker's voice, I knew she didn't have other alternatives. So, we agreed to take her.

We were not expecting the girl who walked in our door. The kids we'd had in the past were beaten down, and their demeanor reflected it. But not the young lady who entered our home. She was tattered and tired, but she had a smile and piercing hazel eyes. She was introduced as Alejandra. Her family was from Sinaloa.

It wasn't long before I was calling her Mija. She and Linda hit it off from the go. Alejandra had no problem with our family structure, and it was evident that she thrived on it rather quickly. All kids need a sense of normalcy, structure, and predictability. It gives them a sense of security. When that breaks down, kids seek normalcy and acceptance in some other group or activity. Unfortunately, those kids are often the ones I meet as adults in the jail system.

But Alejandra was different. For the first couple of days, she called me Ed. Then, I remember one afternoon, she came to me and asked. "I don't want to call you Ed. Can I call you, Dad?"

I hadn't had a bigger smile in a while. "Yes, of course. It would be an honor."

Unlike the other girls who had come through our home, Alejandra had no scheduled meetings with her mother. Alejandra's and her mother's relationship was strange to us. Her mother hadn't even earned enough respect that she would call her "mother," but instead would always refer to her as the "lady." As difficult as that maternal rejection must have been, Alejandra didn't take it out on others in fits of rage and anger, or drugs and alcohol, or aberrant behavior. Instead, Alejandra was a delightful girl, willing to listen, learn, and become part of the family. As far as she was concerned, she wanted to fit into our family life and take advantage of all the love and affection we had to offer. She attended the local high school where she became a good student, developed good friendships, and was well-liked.

We never met her mother, and she never made an effort to see her or have her returned to the family. Other girls came after her and went through the reconciliation process with their families, but not Mija.

Linda and Alejandra became close, and I believe Linda's fondest dream was to have a daughter. Unofficially, she became the daughter Linda had always wanted. Linda had carried a child to near term that she lost in 1995, a daughter, it turned out, who was still born. It was a heartbreaking moment in her life and our married life. I know how much she wanted to raise a daughter alongside our two wonderful sons.

Alejandra's situation with her mother came to a head when a social worker handed her an official document. It was a subpoena to appear in court. Allie was fearful since the social worker hadn't informed her of the nature of the court appearance. We were sure the hearing would be about her mother's parental rights. We didn't know what the mother wanted. As long as Allie had been with us, her mother had not made one move to contact her. Alejandra didn't know what to expect, and neither did we. Linda went with her, and to everyone's surprise, the hearing was short and sweet. Her mother had filed a petition with the court to terminate all her parental rights. And at the concurrence of the Social Services Department, the judge approved it. Mija was on her own. She could decide where she wanted to live, and she chose to stay with us as our daughter. We never officially adopted Alejandra, but in every sense, she became our daughter. We became her legal guardians.

It's interesting to note that if the parents wanted a child returned, and Social Services agreed, the child would have to go. But Alejandra had no interest in pursuing her family, which was made up of stepbrothers and sisters. And her mother never requested to even talk to her. The abuse and neglect must have been ongoing since Allie had no interest in re-entering that world. Allie stayed with us through junior high and high school and a few college years.

Today she is a wonderful mother and wife and is employed as a flight attendant for a major airline. We were so blessed to have her in our home and share God's goodness with her.

Over the years, when people we met found out we had fostered children, they often quipped something like, "Oh, I would do that, but I'm afraid I would get too attached to the child, and then they'd leave."

I thought about that response, and after a while, I figured it was more of an excuse than a legitimate reason. Fostering was never about Linda or me but about the child who came to us broken and hurt. We always focused on what we could do for them; whether their stay with us was long or short, we wanted to leave them with a positive impression of what a loving home felt like. I think it's selfish and self-centered not to get involved only because someone feared getting "too attached." That's making it about you and your feelings. Not about the child and their needs.

Over the five years we fostered, we had twelve kids come through our home, and we gave them the same care and attention we gave our own. I know we made a positive impression on each of them, whether they ran or were returned to their home. We included the kids in everything we were doing: sports, church, doctors, dentists, new clothes, eating pizza, eating out, family events, outings to Disneyland, Knotts Berry Farm; wherever we went, they went with us. If we only accomplished a moment of incremental change in their lives, even in the ones who didn't care to stick around, I believe the experience was worth it, both for them and us.

*

What's true about a department as diverse as L.A. County Sheriff's, is just about any career path one can imagine in law enforcement is open to every deputy who qualifies. Some deputies decide to transfer to the narcotics squad, detectives, or SWAT, but I desired to work with people, particularly youth. When the opportunity arose for me to take up a position at the Youth Activity League (Y.A.L.) in the Lennox section of L.A., I took it. Lennox is in unincorporated county territory, so sheriffs patrol it. The area is primarily Hispanic, while adjacent to it is the Vermont section, primarily a black community. The Sheriff's Department sponsors the Y.A.L. as an after-school alternative. I was elated for the chance to work with kids. It was an ideal situation for me to mentor and teach kids, the explorers, and to teach at the Clergy Academy. I shared duties with several other deputies, and we worked well together, communicating with the kids. I knew the lingo, and I was bilingual, so I fit right in. It didn't take long for the kids who were there regularly to know they could relate to me. My role there wasn't to bust them for being kids but to teach them about the choices they could make in their lives.

Working with the sheriff's explorers was uniquely challenging because those kids wanted to learn more about a career in law enforcement, and they were proud of their choices. The explorers are junior cadets. The kids were all put through a background check, fingerprinted, etc., so they understood the need to stay clear of trouble. They attend a Saturday Academy for 18 weeks, which gives them a basic introduction to the training and bookwork required to be a deputy. Besides the classroom work, they get yelled at as they march and exercise. It was an immersive experience many of the kids thrived on. They also had to maintain a passing grade point average, so it was great to see their progress at report card time. They were proud to show me the fruit of their hard work. My partner and I were good to the kids, and we earned their respect. So, when the kids went to functions, they performed well. They would get to participate in crowd control functions where we could oversee them. It was an excellent opportunity for the kids to learn discipline and accountability. But they had to practice caution. They dare not wear their tan and green uniform home to their neighborhood. The perception on the streets in the minority communities is that deputies are there to bring the hammer of the law down on them any chance they get. I know several of them who went into law enforcement, either as deputies or with local agencies, and they have done very well. Others didn't turn out so well. But then that's what we emphasized—their futures rested in their hands and the choices they made every day. Life is about choices: The same door of opportunity existed for all of them, but it was up to them to walk through it.

*

I would get loaned (CARP) out to the station to do patrol work or as the jailer in Lennox. On patrol, you're always dealing with the tensions and concerns of the neighborhoods we police. So, it's always important to know how to defuse tensions, to walk that fine line between the letter of the law that penalizes every infraction, and the spirit of the law that gains people's trust and gets them to willingly comply with the law, for their safety and well-being.

One time I was working in the Lennox area, a section of L.A. County adjacent to Compton. I pulled over a vehicle for speeding. His car had sped through a section of streets full of houses near a school. The first thing he said to me when I reached his window.

"You pulled me over because I'm black."

"No, I didn't pull you over because you're black."

"Yeah, you did."

I thought for a moment, "Okay, I'm going to stand here for two minutes, and we're going to count all the white people that drive by."

"Come on, deputy, man. You know there are no white people around here."

"Exactly! Why would you something like that? This is a 25-mph residential area, and you were going 40. Do you know how hard it is to stop if little Jonny chases a ball into the street?"

"Yeah, well, you know how it is right now, man."

"No, I don't know how it is. Don't play with me like that."

He looked at me kind of sheepishly.

"Look, I got a job to do protecting the neighborhood. That's what I do. So slow down, man."

"Okay, deputy, I apologize."

That was the end of that. The letter of the law says, "Fool, you're getting one. Press hard for all three copies." But I didn't go there. I let him off with a warning, and he seemed grateful. He wanted to be a victim, but I refused to take the bait. I believe the spirit of the law is as valuable to practice as the letter. I took every opportunity to send the right message that we aren't looking to fill our jails. We have a job to do—protect our neighborhoods, make the streets safe for everyone. The vast majority of sheriff's deputies do that every day; they serve with excellence, and I had the absolute good fortune to learn from and to work with the best of them.

*

It's not always easy to keep your cool, but it's something I always worked on, taking a deep breath before acting or talking. But there are moments when a little righteous indignation can go a long way. But one must be careful.

One evening shift, I was working on loan to the Lennox Station, serving as the jailer. A juvenile had been picked up for violating curfew and was in the holding tank. It was my job to call his parents to come to pick him up. He lived with his mother, who didn't speak English and didn't have a vehicle. I'm sure she worked as a laborer. She came to the station by taxi, which meant she spent more money she probably couldn't afford. When I was checking out the young man, I returned his money to his mother, and she took and counted it. I could see disappointment register on her face.

She asked in Spanish. "Where's the rest of the money? That's rent money? Where is it?"

Her son responded, "Shut up, puta."

I couldn't believe what he had just called his mother. I was so furious that I grabbed him by his shirt collar and dragged him through the station's lobby. I kicked the door open and flung him outside. I pointed at him, "There are two places for you, death or prison. I know I'm going to see you again."

His mother came up behind me and said in Spanish, "Thank you for doing that." Inside the station, the watch commander was all over me. "Ed, Ed that is against policy." I knew it was, but he had so infuriated me, I had to throw him out the front doors of the station. Hopefully, it knocked some sense into him.

I told the Lieutenant what he had called his mother. He didn't know Spanish, so he didn't understand the derogatory nature of puta. The watch commander said, "What?"

"Yeah, he called his mother a prostitute." I apologized to him. He could have written me up for it, but he decided not to, considering what the boy had said. The only gratifying thing about the whole episode was that the boy's mother found me and thanked me for shaking him up like that.

Respect for authority begins with honoring parents and learning to respect the authority figures in kids' lives. Teaching kids to respect their parents is worth more than just about anything else a parent could teach them or bequeath them because it sets them up for success in so many ways.

Many single mothers are at their wit's end on what to do with strong-willed kids who don't want to listen to them. One day, a distraught mother brought her son to the Y.A.L. and asked me to speak some sense into him. I took the young man aside and counseled him, telling him that he needed to put himself under the authority of his mother. Doing so would protect him and keep him out of the vast amount of trouble stalking his neighborhood.

"Putting yourself under your mother's authority, listening to her, and doing what she says, will earn you your freedom as an adult. The alternative is you don't do that, and someday your freedom will be taken from you, and you'll come to me in the jails. There you'll be under my authority, and you won't like it. I'll tell you what to wear, when to sleep, when to eat, what you can read, who you can talk to. I'll control every aspect of your life, and you won't like it."

It seemed to make a difference in the young man, and I hope the lesson stayed with him.*

One of the joys of working with students took me to Washington Preparatory High School, where I taught student and law. I remember having a conversation with the school principal. She told me that 90 percent of the high school kids were in secondary homes—grandparents, aunts, uncles, or other relatives. The community suffers from a lack of attention and credible role models among the adults they know. The opportunity to be a role model to kids who had few credible role models was one of the high points of my time at the Y.A.L.

A great experience, I emphasized with the students that the role of the police wasn't to bust heads but to preserve the peace. I found teaching to be a very satisfying experience, and the kids and I bonded to the point they thought I was "cool." I don't believe that being arrogant about your authority is the duty of a peace officer.

After completing one of my classes, the kids presented me with a large card thanking me for my time with them.

They thought I was "cool." Being cool didn't mean permissive, but it meant that I knew how to relate to them in a way they could understand. The law wasn't out to get them; it was there to protect them. I will never compromise the message that has served me and many others well: "The fear of the Lord is the beginning of Wisdom..." (Prov. 9:10). I couldn't speak to them directly about the Lord, but I could tell them about how respect for authority in their lives would set them up for success. The laws and rules our society set out only penalize the arrogant and stupid who don't see value in being respectful of authority.

I also set them straight on judging all police officers and deputies by the bad examples of the sensationalized few on the news. I would often use a simple analogy.

"Okay, so here are the class rules. If I catch one of you cheating, you all flunk the class. A big fat 'F' for each one of you."

This immediately raises the hackles of kids who are fine-tuned to what's fair and not so fair. The kids instinctually know this would be unfair to judge an entire class by the irresponsible actions of one student. Once they agreed that would be an unacceptable rule, I asked them why they judged all police on the errors and misjudgments of the few. And it is the few by far. Not all deputies and police officers are bad. In my book, the vast majority willingly strap on their equipment each day to protect and serve. The worst part of my job was being judged along with the bad officers who crossed the line. The media attention to the bad apples becomes problematic to the entire force, but I don't believe it ever deterred the good guys from doing their jobs. We do it despite the bad press, despite the chances of being misunderstood and mistrusted. Much more could be accomplished in our communities across our nation if more trust existed between the police and the public they served.

One of the stories I often told my students was the time I was working overtime in the Norwalk Superior Courts. One of the duties of the sheriff's department is security in the courts, bailiffs in the courtroom, and escorting prisoners in and out of the courtroom before and after their cases are heard. On this occasion, we had a prisoner who was designated a "keep away." He was a bad dude, a violent offender, and a notorious member of the Mexican Mafia. He was housed in a single man cell with a hard door while he waited his turn. When the courtroom bailiff informed me "he's up," I opened the hard door, and spoke to him through the barred door. It was his turn to go.

It's a small cell, with a bench along the wall, and he was sitting, bare chested in the stuffy room. He stood, and turned his back to me, and while he retrieved his shirt, his tattoo, scrolled across his back amazed me. Not in the sense that it was evil in any way. I'd seen plenty of those. But its cryptic honesty.

It read, "I HAD A CHOICE."

He buttoned his shirt, stepped to the door, and presented his hands for me to chain him. A high security prisoner, I cuffed him with waist chains, a chain that wraps around the waist and secures the wrists. It limits the range of motion prisoners can move their hands away from their bodies.

As I escorted him down the hall to the courtroom, my curiosity wouldn't let me remain silent. I had to ask him.

"Sir, I have to ask you. What's the meaning of that tattoo on your back?"

He gave a soft sigh and nodded. "Yeah, you know deputy, people want to blame their parents, or society, and even you guys for our problems." He turned his head to me as he shuffled down the hall. "I chose this path; no one forced me. I'm not a victim, deputy." And with that we proceeded to courtroom.

I was stunned by his revelation, his honesty, and his willingness to take responsibility for his decision to associate himself with the most violent criminal element. I respected him in that moment, not for his evil deeds, or the reputation for violence he had gained, but for his acknowledgement of his own culpability in his life of crime. He knew it was an evil path, and he chose it for his own set of reasons.

I believe there is a general misconception that crime and criminals are victims of poverty and bad parenting and even bad policing. Certainly, parenting and the school system and the environment play a crucial role in the formation of young people's character and choices, but at the end of the day individuals are responsible for their choices.

8

Leaving My First Love, Jesus

My family troubles began as niggling of unhappiness at home, an annoyance that I allowed to boil over into full-blown resentment that almost destroyed my relationship with Linda and my kids. I'm not making excuses; I'm being honest. But one who cherished his life under authority, there came a time when I consciously put that thinking in my rearview mirror and headed out into uncharted territory, at least for me anyway. By uncharted, I mean a life of open sin. I call it that because that's what it was. I believed a lie for a period in my life; I not only believed it, but lived it, enjoyed it, and thought this was my future. I deserved to have some fun; I had worked hard and built a career. But all I can say is pleasure is so deceitful, it played me for a Fool.

As I reflect on the roots of what ended up being twelve years of struggle, I believe it started with stepping out from under God's authority. I had always been a man who respected the book, the Word of God, and the book of laws. I lived by a code as a deputy and as a husband and father. But I allowed myself to slip away from the influence and authority of God and the Holy Spirit.

I believe it started with a split in the church we were attending. The pastors disagreed, and I honestly don't remember what the argument was over. The group we followed ended up going in the wrong direction, doctrinally. For the first time, we lost touch with a church family. With my struggles at home and the hours I worked, I didn't try to find a new church home. During the last year or so, I was going through the motions at church. I had lost my engagement with the Bible and Holy Spirit. These were gradual steps that I believe that was the first step in my downward spiral.

Then, drinking with the guys, I began to give into temptations and a false narrative that came right from the pit of hell.

You were too young to get married.

She wasn't meant for you.

Many thoughts like this became my reality. It's difficult, looking back, to talk about how deeply I believed the lies and falsehoods of the enemy, but I did. I allowed myself to be deluded that my marriage didn't matter, my family didn't matter, and that God's word was negotiable.

*

When I learned that the position for a Bonus Deputy at Twin Towers opened up, I took the test and sat for an interview. I had ten years now with the department, and after testing and an in-person interview, I qualified for a promotion to a two-striper or a corporal. So, I was slotted into the bonus deputy position at Twin Towers. This was a supervisory assignment, working about 60 to 80 deputies coming in from the academy just as I had a decade before.

I enjoyed working with the young guys, and gals, they had genuine respect for my experience and insight and respected my leadership. With the copious overtime and young guys looking up to me for guidance, training, and everyday wisdom at being a good deputy, I had found a group that appreciated me.

As I became immersed in working at the Twin Towers, working many 16-hour days, we had saved enough to purchase a home that would serve all our needs—for both our kids and foster kids. While I worked more, Linda wasn't slowing down. She was busy—kid's activities, parent and social worker visits with foster kids, the new home, her church, and more. We continued to miss each other, and my resentment grew into open rebellion.

At work, I threw myself into the job.

The Twin Towers is unlike any other jail in the L.A. County system, for that matter in the country. It was built as a state-of-the-art jail and opened in 1997. It uses a unique panoptic design that allows deputies sitting in a central control room to monitor cells by looking right through the optically transparent material. Deputies still had to do their safety checks but didn't have to open cells to observe. We used to do inspections every 30 minutes, but because of several undetected incidents, such as a suicide, we now do cell checks every 15 minutes.

The department's need for such a facility continues to grow as the population of prisoners with mental health issues explodes. Every year, the number of mental health cases held in the Twin Towers increases with no reduction in sight. The department has taken steps to integrate complementary county services such as the mental health department staff, social workers from social services, and housing and medical experts to meet the needs of the individuals coming through the jail system. Many of them are suffering debilitation mental issues that prohibit them from holding regular jobs. Homelessness isn't a crime, but in their struggle for survival on the streets, they often commit crimes that get them a warm, safe place to sleep, meds administered on schedule, and three meals. Some of them are openly reluctant to leave once their release date arrives.

The awareness of mental health issues has taken on a critical role in deputy's training as well. For example, when I was in the academy in the early '90s, we had no training in mental health issues; now, the training has been extended two weeks and is dedicated to identifying and dealing with citizens going through a mental crisis.

With my move to the Twin Towers, I began working more overtime to save enough to purchase a bigger house. Unfortunately, it worked against us financially for Linda to continue her part-time job at UPS. With her home full time, we were able to begin fostering kids, and she took on a much more significant role in caring for our two, plus the ones who came into our home.

Linda became absorbed in the life of the kids. When I came home, they were gone. Or during my free time, when I had time off, they were off to Disneyland, or a school or sports function, events I couldn't attend because they conflicted with my work schedule. Linda and the kids were running on a completely different life schedule, and it began to wear on me. At first, I was annoyed at being left out of the family activities. But the reality of the situation was that I had chosen to work these hours, and I thrived on working. That didn't change how I felt. I was going one way, and they were headed in another direction.

I grew up in a home where no one talked about what bothered them. In my large family, we weren't all one happy family. There was conflict, hurt feelings, disappointments, but they were never brought out into the open. And no yelling or back was talking to each other. I brought this habit into my relationship with Linda. We never argued or cussed at each other or even said, "shut up." Instead, we showed each other, at least outwardly, mutual respect. I was unhappy with our home life, and we never had a sit-down session where we tried to hash out our feelings.

It wasn't something we did.

I was unhappy, feeling left out, underappreciated, and, frankly, not valued for the hard work and financial stability I brought to the family. With my resentment festering,

I opened myself up to solutions that only hardened my heart toward home, family, and God. I did something that had been unthinkable in our relationship, our home, or our lives.

I began drinking and hanging out with the guys.

With only an empty house to go home to, I began hanging out with the guys after shifts. We'd meet at a local bar, a restaurant, or in the parking lot of the Twin Towers. I was thirty-three years old, and I never drank alcohol, smoked anything, or hung out with those who did. But there I was, a veteran supervisor of men, in the parking lot, or wherever we met, knocking back beer after beer, with these 20-something guys. I was an authoritative voice, and I gladly took them under my wings and showed them the ropes. Here was a group of guys, among whom I could do no wrong—I was like a cool uncle. And I loved it.

What others might call drinking parties, we called debriefing or choir practice—a vital training tool, I reasoned, that was unlike the classroom work we were all used to. We could get so much more done over beer and whiskey sours than we could be hammering through the policy manual. Often women came to our drinking sessions regularly. Wherever we happened to be—gals would find us. We called our group, The Choir Boys. There was nothing saintly about our meetings. Among the perks of hanging out with young and frisky men were the hang-on girls. We called them Donut Dollies and Badge Bunnies. I don't know how they found us, but they knew where we met and when.

I was having fun and making money and not paying much attention to God, my family, or caring for my spiritual life in any way. I stopped attending church and reading my Bible. It doesn't take long to travel a great distance in your heart from the God who speaks in the quiet moments. I had no quiet moments any longer. When my anger, resentment, or conscience would rear its head, I had a beer, or two, or three. Whatever it took.

I began to live a life of 'I wanted what I wanted.' And I wanted a bigger and better house, one I could have my friends over and enjoy some relaxation. So, since Linda wasn't paying attention to me, I searched for a place myself. I found our Whittier house, made an offer, and then brought Linda over to see it.

She was angry. She didn't want to move, and she made up every reason imaginable for why we shouldn't move. I gave her no option. We were moving, and that was that. She came to enjoy the new place, but that didn't mean she had to be happy with having no say in it. Frankly, I didn't care about her feelings. It was obvious to me, she cared little for mine.

In time, the new home convinced her. It was much more spacious with three bedrooms, two and a half baths, and manicured backyard with a pool that would get a lot of use by the kids and foster children who came through.

I had plans for it as well.

We were living in different worlds. She knew nothing

of my friends, of my fellow deputies, of the men I led and trained. Until one day, I brought them home after a shift to lounge in the pool and drink.

As these things go, one thing led to another. The relationship between Linda and I took a wrong turn. She wasn't listening to me, and I wasn't listening to her. We moved despite her objections. Emotionally, we were as far apart as two people can be and still live under one roof.

One afternoon, the tension came to a head when she arrived home early and found three off duty deputies and me lounging in our pool, drinking beers. She was shocked; I could see it, to witness me drinking and hanging out with friends. But admittedly, it wasn't something I had ever done before. I didn't bring friends home. I didn't have any hobbies outside of work.

We had our first loud fight in our entire marriage. The words flew, thick and blue. I was so upset at her reaction to my idea of a bit of recreation, I decided that was it—I was leaving. I packed an overnight bag while she stood by, asking me what I was doing. I sensed the fear in her voice - good, I thought. She deserved to be afraid, treating me like I was some kid who was far too young to have a beer with friends.

My leaving was a pure selfish impulse. I bunked on a buddy's sofa for a few weeks, hoping it would inject some reality into her stick-in-the-mud attitude. I knew our separation wasn't the best situation for either one of us or the kids. But I needed some time to let my simmering resentment subside. We talked several times on the phone, and she sounded conciliatory. So, after a few weeks, I returned home, hoping the tension had eased.

Unfortunately, while the kids were glad to see me, Linda was too busy to give me much attention. Granted, she had her hands full with two active boys and foster kids coming and going.

We were ships passing in the fog.

In 2005, I transferred to a recruiting position in personnel. The department needed to staff up and anticipated hiring 1,200 new deputies in the next three years. The recruitment department staffed up with twenty-four sworn deputies and custody assistants. We needed the staff because of the requirements to recruit, interview, and assist in processing the volumes of applications for potential recruits. The process was rigorous. Over the next three years, we generated 20,000 applicants to meet our goals. Recruiting required travel, a lot of public speaking, and constant interaction with potential recruits. I loved meeting people and talking to them about my favorite subject, law enforcement in general and the sheriff's department in particular. I polished my public speaking skills and learned to enjoy standing in front of an audience. Selling the benefits of a career in law enforcement at job fairs, on college campuses, and in classrooms became second nature. We made junkets to Las Vegas for giant job fairs and college campuses across the nation. As the nation's largest sheriff's department, with the most extensive jail system, we covered the country looking for qualified candidates.

In three years, we met our goal of hiring 1,200 deputies. The mammoth task required us to hire over thirty new deputies a month, filling new classes at the academy every quarter.

With no resolution to our ongoing disagreements, I moved out permanently and moved in with one of my brothers. I began living a self-indulgent life. Eventually, I rented an apartment by the beach and became a philanderer. The way I saw it was I wasn't living at home as a married man, and I was now single. I didn't see any problem denying my marriage vows. I was in and out of relationships, and it didn't bother me in the slightest. My spiritual life was at an extremely low point. If you met me on the street or in a bar, you'd have every reason to believe I was just another heathen, enjoying his hedonistic lifestyle.

By 2008, the recruiting department had met our hiring goals. With the economy falling off a cliff and housing and employment spiraling into a steep decline, the team members began to transfer out. When the department's new budget was released, and a hiring freeze was put in place, it didn't take much prodding to see the writing on the wall. I decided to return to a supervisory slot at the Twin Towers. For the next eight years, I worked as a bonus deputy at the Twin Towers, completing my career of twenty-five years with the sheriff's department.

About this time, I wanted to end my charade of a marriage, and I filed for a divorce. We were married in name only. I rarely saw Linda or the kids, though I ensured she had the money she needed to keep the house and give the kids what they needed. Thankfully, an event took place that gave me occasion to reconsider my decision to pursue a divorce. My youngest son was graduating from eighth grade, and graduations are a big family event; my siblings and nieces and nephews would be in attendance. I showed up and watched my son receive his eighth-grade diploma. Seeing my kids and Linda turned me around; though it didn't solve my problem, it softened my hardened heart. My kids and wife were beautiful, and it struck me that I was willing to give all this up, for what? A fling, a barely furnished apartment, and some drinking buddies. I had regrets, but I still had a hard heart and many issues to resolve before I'd make a good husband and father again.

After that afternoon with my family, I decided to call off the divorce. I had been in and out of the home several times, and I knew it would not work just to move home. Besides, Linda didn't want me to return cold turkey, just show up on the doorstep and announce, "I'm home." But I did stop the divorce proceedings.

I had no idea how to get out of my spiritual state, for I was far from the Lord, but seeing the kids had provided a turning point in my life. I wanted to see them more and began showing up at the house.

During one visit, Linda told me about a new church she was attending. The pastor had helped her, and she thought I would enjoy attending with the kids and her.

I thought, why not? Church hadn't been on my radar

for a few years, but it wouldn't hurt to go with her. Wanting to find a way out of my mess, I had no power within myself to make the needed changes. Nor did I understand what changes had to be made. There existed no clear idea in my mind what had to be done, but I knew I was in a bad place. Anger dominated my inner life and motivation, but I never saw it as anger. And worse of all, I didn't understand why I was angry.

For a few months, I moved home. Linda wanted me back in the house, and I wanted to return. It was great to be around the kids, but there was a part of me that was far, far from the man I once was—a devoted husband and father. While there was no more philandering, I was still drinking and hanging out with the Choir Boys. Drinking had become my medication, my pain reliever, my way of anesthetizing myself to the grossness inside that festered and wanted to be free of the constraints of family responsibilities.

I moved out in 2012, wanting to be rejoin my friends and the world of self-indulgence.

That was it for Linda. Sometime that year, she decided it was her turn to end the charade of our marriage. She had enough of my acting out and filed for divorce. I remember the day a man served the papers. Holding them in my hand at the apartment door, the realization she meant business swept through me. Was this the last chance to save my marriage? Did I just forget it and let go? Deep inside, I wanted to find a way back, to return to her love, and the love and joy of my children. I missed them the way a man often misses the best parts of himself.

I was a man torn, living between two worlds that were rapidly moving apart. Decisions were pending that would become irreversible. I was a lost soul, drifting along, caught in the current of my own pleasures and selfishness.

At one time, I remembered, there existed an anchor in my life, but I had loosed those mooring ropes long ago. They felt lost to me now. I needed help. But there is a truth about being a man of authority, used to giving orders, and enforcing laws—it's hard to bow the head; it's difficult to ask for help. Thoughts of reaching out to another continued to grind on a part of me that refused to give up my pleasures, my way of doing things. The pride of life ruled me. It didn't seem possible to find a way out of my predicament.

9

Linda's Story

LINDA ROMAN

The fracture in our marriage had been widening for several years, and it finally broke open one afternoon when I came home and Ed and a few of his deputy co-workers were drinking in our backyard, something he had never done before. We had just moved into a lovely new home in Whittier, with three bedrooms, a pool, and more space for our two growing boys and foster children. I had been out all day, doing errands, and taking care of the boys and our foster kids, feeling a bit angry when I arrived home to find Ed and three of his deputy buddies in our backyard, laughing, and most alarming of all, drinking. In our twelve years of marriage, I had never seen him take one sip of alcohol. And now empty beer bottles were on the deck.

My reaction was pure outrage. Admittedly, I was rude to him and his friends. After the men left, Ed and I had the first loud argument of our marriage. There had never been any shouting or name-calling between us. We had never cussed or told each other to "shut up." But the argument that day was raw and direct. In my mind, Who was this man? We were church-going people. We didn't drink or cuss or fool around. But, in reality, we were both far from God in our hearts. Attending church had become a formality, a habit that allowed me to check a box, and then I could tell myself all was well with God.

But all was far from well, not only in my relationship with Ed but with the Lord. After our argument, he went into our bedroom and began packing an overnight bag. I stood and watched him in disbelief and filled with fear, not realizing his plan. He was our family's faithful, consistent rock, always there behind the scenes, working hard and longing to make a better life for all of us. But he hadn't been present for some time, shifting silently into the background. I had accepted his lack of engagement in the family, but not this, not him packing a bag. When I asked him what he was doing, he told me he was leaving. He said, "I'm done! I'm tired of you not appreciating me, and I want out."

He went on to say, he didn't feel welcome any longer in our home.

His words sent a shock through me. I had to take a breath to catch myself. What had I done? I hadn't meant to push him so far that he would leave. I didn't understand his drinking and wanting to be around his friends than with his family. He had never brought any of these friends home, and I had never met any of these men before. Now to see these men and Ed in our pool, drinking and carrying on, I had flipped out. But it was the drinking that my mind focused on at that moment. Something as Christians we hadn't done, didn't do, didn't think we should be doing. Why didn't Ed understand that?

Ed left the house that night, and when the door closed behind him, I sat on our sofa, and a dread of fear washed over me. I knew we were in trouble. But it was an unnamed trouble. I had never imagined he would leave our home, other than the argument over his buddies drinking in our backyard. Ed never talked about the stress he endured at work, and I had no idea of the struggles he was having. Then there were my issues. If you asked me that day, I couldn't put my finger on why I had erupted like that. The thing about anger is it doesn't truly express the most profound issues. It only took the top off a deep emotional cauldron of resentment bubbling up inside me. I had worked nonstop to take care of my responsibilities, and he's living it up with these men. But there were other issues in play, deeper ones.

If a devoted wife and mother was oblivious to her husband's struggles, I was a poster child for that obliviousness. There was so much I didn't understand about Ed's struggles and needs. Only after years of trials, struggles, prayer, and counseling did we find each other again. To discover who we were as children of God, servants of Christ, and the true meaning of God's love and forgiveness. Every step of the journey was painful but necessary. For me, it was a journey to discover the true meaning of surrendering to Christ. Neither one of us had surrendered to Christ; neither one of us was allowing God to speak to us and to use our lives for His purpose. Both of us were stuck in our own worlds.

That said, my journey began with the realization that I had become a self-absorbed woman. This wasn't a conscious choice, but one I believed was justified by the demands of our home and children. Besides, I had struggles of my own with my sense of purpose and worth to maintain, and that effort hadn't included Ed for the past few years.

Only the shock of Ed's leaving forced me to reflect, but it didn't change me at that moment. But with Ed gone, I did begin to evaluate how our marriage had reached such a low point, one that threatened to break us apart. How could this happen?

With two children and two foster children to care for, my life had narrowed down to the concerns of the children and home. Ed was working long hours because he wanted a better life for us, but he became nearly invisible in the home. Ed had wanted me to quit my part-time job at UPS, which I loved, because it didn't make sense for us financially. With me away from home, it deprived Ed of the opportunity to work the more lucrative over time with the sheriff's department. My job had been a puzzle piece to my identity and sense of self-worth, and with that gone, I threw myself into the role of the stay-at-home mom, who didn't enjoy staying at home 24/7.

I became a room mother at my son's school; I carted

the kids around town for their activities; and kept a full schedule of regular meetings the Social Services Department required of foster parents. The goal of fostering was to help the children reconcile with their parents or immediate family, eventually returning home. That meant constant monitored visits at coffee shops, libraries, or any convenient location for a social worker, parent, or guardians. Children coming into our home often hadn't seen a doctor or dentist in months, perhaps years, sometimes never. They needed new clothes or other services, and I was responsible for seeing that they received them.

While I was living my life, I didn't understand fully how much Ed had become entangled in a life of his own, one apart from the family and me. Ed never opened up to me, and it never occurred to me to ask him. I knew of his restlessness for several years. He constantly wanted more—a better house, a more exotic vacation, a new boat, a better car, always more and better things for us. He also wanted a larger home, and he took it upon himself to find one in Whitter, a spacious three bedroom with a pool. By the time he thought to bring me to see it, he had already made an offer and made arrangements for the mortgage. I resented the idea of moving because I knew the lion's share of the work would fall on my shoulders. Even though I admired the new home, I didn't dare tell him that. I had my grievances to nurse. By the time we moved into our Whittier home with the pool, we had been disconnected emotionally. Honestly, I didn't realize the cruel seriousness of how far our marriage had deteriorated, how far apart we had grown in our friends and habits until the incident with his friends in our back yard.

And now Ed was gone. I was feeling so many things, and it wasn't easy to sort them out. I was bitter and resentful that I had to carry the entire load of the house and boys and foster children. I was giving and giving and giving, and Ed worked constantly or was out with his friends having a good time. It was difficult for me to get past my hard feelings over my situation, but I wanted Ed to come home. I wanted to change, but I didn't know how.

Over the next two weeks, we phoned each other, talking about our situation. I told him I wanted him to come home. I wanted to do anything to get him back. My greatest fear was that he wouldn't return. I knew he was unhappy, but I didn't know what to do about it. I didn't know anything about his drinking. I was deeply resentful and bitter that he couldn't understand what I was dealing with, how heavy a load I was carrying with the entire burden of home and children on my shoulders.

When he returned, we fell back into our regular routines, which was catastrophic for our marriage. He was on high alert for my attitude, and it hadn't changed even though I worked hard, or thought I did, to be more accommodating to him. I tried to change and not let my bad attitude show, but I couldn't transform overnight. Any little thing I said or did that he didn't like, he wouldn't put up with. I didn't understand then that he felt unappreciated, unloved, and not needed. We conversed, but not on the level necessary to solve our problems. Nothing was going to change in either of us until we were willing to take a deep look at ourselves. He had a plan if things didn't work out at home. I had no idea that he had a group of friends who became his drinking buddies. Within a few months, he moved out again—with a suitcase. His way of dealing with his frustration was to escape. Escape to a place where he had friends, and to what I would only find out later, were drinking escapes.

He stayed with his brother and told me he had no plans to return. I was devastated at the news. I wanted him to return, and I tried to do everything I could to get him to come home. But he refused. I pleaded with him to come home, but nothing I said or promised worked. As far as he was concerned, our marriage was over. He was off having fun and didn't want to put any work into saving our marriage. In looking back, I can thank God he didn't return just then. He wasn't ready to change, and I hadn't begun to look into my contribution to the dissolution of our marriage.

His decision to leave us shook me hard enough that I began to reach out for an answer. One day in my living room, after my mother had picked up the kids so she could visit with them, I cried out to God for help. It occurred to me that our next-door neighbor was a pastor. I went to see him, and our conversation was the beginning of my path to healing.

My conversation with my neighbor, Mr. Smotherman was the most enlightening and convicting one I had ever had. He pointed out that we both had a spiritual problem, and I had to explore my contribution to our breakup in prayer. I couldn't change Ed; I had to experience a change in my own life and pray the same happened in Ed's life.

I remember going home with an understanding and hope at what I'd just heard. But, of course, God had the answer, if I wanted to hear it. The house was quiet with the kids gone. I knelt in the living room, alone with God, and I cried out to Him:

Please, God, show me who I have been and how I got here.

I heard Him say, Are you sure?

Yes, God, I want to know.

It was a profound moment; the memory of it still lingers with me. After agreeing that I wanted to know the truth, the Holy Spirit stripped away the top layer of my superficial concerns. Images and faces began flashing before my eyes, glimpsing for the first time my true self: I felt entitled; I wasn't appreciative of all the good things Ed did for us; I had made friends with women who weren't good for me, ones who were always telling me what a good man did and didn't do. I had many outside influences that weren't healthy for me and my marriage. Most fundamental of all, I had been raised by strong women who knew how to take control and take care of everything. I couldn't control everything; I could only surrender myself to Christ and walk in His ways. It was a terrifying and revealing day, God showing me that I had worked hard over the years to tear down my husband and our marriage. None of my issues exonerated Ed and his decision to escape the home, but neither did it exonerate me. Ed had his deep-seated problems to address, and it would take him years to realize what he was dealing with. But God had made my task clear. I was to work on my issues, get my heart right with God, and be the woman and mother God intended me to be.

That day in my living room, I surrendered my heart, my will, my mind, and my emotions to Christ. Something I hadn't done entirely before. I no longer wanted to be a churchgoer, but I wanted to be committed follower of Christ, wherever that took me. I willingly accepted that He was in control of my life, my marriage, and my children. From that day on, I sought God and His direction and wisdom for my life and family. I searched out resources to help me better understand what I needed to do. I realized I needed to surround myself with Godly women and a good church who could positively influence me and support me through these challenging times. I also decided to begin attending seeing a counselor I knew was focused on marriage.

I wanted Ed back; I wanted my marriage to be restored; I wanted peace in our home. But I knew now that none of these things would happen if I tried to make it happen in my power. I needed the transforming work of totally surrendering to Christ and living in that reality each day. My greatest desire was to have my marriage back, but God made clear to me that I needed to die to the old Linda, the

Linda that had to be in control and harbored resentments and anger at my husband. I had to die to the old Linda.

Through my prayer time, I believe God spoke to me about what it would take to get my marriage back, that I wouldn't be any good for Ed, my children, and myself if I didn't get healing from my past. I don't remember how I found it, but I began reading Stormie Omartian's book, Lord, I Want to Be Whole.[9] I began to heal emotionally as I prayed and read Scripture. I was beginning to experience freedom from my emotional baggage. The second resource that helped me grow was Total Forgiveness, by R.T. Kendall.[10]

And I would have to forgive him, and I didn't even realize then how much I would have to forgive him for. But, as difficult as that seemed, the real difficulty was forgiving myself. If I could accept God's forgiveness for how I had injured my husband, I could extend God's forgiveness and acceptance to Ed, and that for me was the true beginning of the healing in my life and in our relationship. These two books gave me a complete view of myself and where I had been emotionally and gave me insight into the healing and forgiving journey I needed to take.

Forgiveness has taken the longest because it's experienced in steps, at least for me. I understood the need to forgive Ed and his actions. The most difficult challenge was forgiving myself. I remember reading passages of the

9 Stormie Omartian, Lord, I Want to Be Whole: The Power of Prayer And Scripture in Emotional Healing. Thomas Nelson, 2001
10 R.T. Kendall. Total Forgiveness. Charisma House, 2007

book and then closing it and telling God, Lord, I'm not even ready to forgive myself. Forgiving myself was the most difficult step, because I didn't believe I deserved it. I had become caught up in myself, so that I had lost all appreciation for the husband God gave me. I had lost sight of the man he was when we first met and who he was in the first years in the department. I had no idea what he had endured during all those years working in the jails. True to his character, a trait that complicated my understanding of him, Ed is a silent man. He never brought his work home with him. When he came home, he wasn't Deputy Roman, who had just worked with some of the most dangerous criminals in the city. He was just Ed. That was a decision he made for our family, but ultimately it worked against both of us because he internalized everything.

Ed always wanted to do the right thing for people. He strived never to mistreat anyone just because he was a deputy with all this authority. However, bringing his Christian values with him into the jails put a lot of pressure on him. I had no idea how much pressure he endured as a Christian. His values often isolated him from his fellow deputies because of how he treated the inmates. He refused to be abusive and angry with the inmates, even if they deserved it. His reputation for his kindness and caring put a lot of pressure on him. One story I do remember that illustrates the Ed I know, and love is the time a mother drove all the way from Texas, over fifteen hours, to see her son, but visiting hours were over, and a deputy told her, "It's after hours; it's too late." Ed heard this exchange, and he intervened, pleading with the other deputy, "Hey, she just drove 15 hours to see her son, give her 15 minutes."

The deputy did allow the mother a short visit with her son. But Ed received a lot of criticism for doing that. That's the Ed I know and love. He wanted to do the right thing and treat the inmates with respect, which wasn't always cool with the other deputies. He didn't quite fit in. So, this put a lot of pressure on him not to conform to compromise his values. Then he came home where I had no idea what he was going through. It just wasn't like him to complain until that fateful argument at our home.

Ed and I came from completely different home environments. In Ed's family, no one ever talked about issues or confronted each other, besides the few times, his father called him out or chastised him. He had a lonely upbringing with all his siblings gone from the home by the time he reached elementary school. In my case, I grew up in a home of strong women. My mother was a take-charge lady who got things done, and she would confront any of us children if we weren't meeting her expectations.

Work for Ed was demanding and negative, dealing with the worst element. He fought himself to stay above water emotionally and spiritually, always concerned about doing the right thing. And then he came home, and I could be confronting, controlling, and demanding. The criticism went right to his core sense of self—he didn't feel loved and appreciated. Then when he began hanging around with drinking buddies and drinking with them, I didn't recognize that Ed. So, when it came to forgiving Ed, I didn't have a problem because I had become part of his problem.

Healing emotionally and learning to forgive changed me from the inside out truly. It also allowed me to see Ed the way God saw him. I knew him as the kind and caring husband and dedicated family man I had married. Not the angry man who now spent his free time drinking and going to bars. I didn't recognize the man he had become, but I knew the man he once was, and I began to fight for him. Not physically, but spiritually.

I remember Ed would come over to pick the boys to spend time with him. He'd come into the house and sit, and we'd talk.

Before he left, I'd always tell him, "I'm praying for you."

He would respond with something like, "This is who I am. I like who I am."

"That's not you. I know who you are."

He would shrug and leave.

I know that was the spirit speaking through me. God showed me that Ed was struggling with the ugly parts of his life; evil wanted to take him over completely. The more I realized this, the more I had to fight for him in prayer. In my prayer time, I sensed God telling me to fight for him, to believe He was working out Ed's salvation, but it would take time. I would see more ugliness from Ed, but I had to trust that God was working in his life even when I didn't see it.

God was working in my life as well, giving me peace and understanding in this difficult situation. When Ed came around to see the boys, I believe he noticed the peace God had given me. I wasn't angry and condemning, and I wasn't confrontational. On several occasions, he said he wanted to come home, and I would let him.

I sensed God saying he wasn't ready. But I often argued with that, thinking, No, he's better.

But he wasn't. He came home, but he was unhappy because home life chafed at his lifestyle of drinking and carousing. He would tell me he was working, but he was hanging out with his drinking buddies and girlfriends. Then he would leave when we were gone, so we never saw him pack or try to explain himself. I knew it wasn't good, but I didn't know what to do or handle the situation.

One of my friends told me he had seen him with another woman, so I confronted him. I remember telling him that if that's the life he wanted, I couldn't have him in the home if he wanted that lifestyle. I had to put a boundary. Allowing him to come home when he felt lonely only made it easier for him to live in both of his worlds. He would have to choose for us if he wanted to have a marriage. His struggles holding him back from committing fully to his family were too strong for him to overcome. And his poor choices were causing me a lot of pain. I remember telling God, "I don't hate him, but I don't want to do this anymore." I know he loves the kids, and in some way, he still loves me, but his other life was too much of a pull on him. I believe I had biblical grounds for a divorce, and I thought it was time to move forward. I had to protect my children. Ed's in and out of the home had been dragging on nine years now, and it had to come to an end sometime since Ed didn't know what he wanted.

There were times he would come over, and I could just tell he was lost. He didn't know what to do with his life.

So, I filed for a divorce.

I was preparing for a life as a single mother, which I already had been the last nine years, but I knew that I would need to return to work. So, I found employment nearby in Santa Fe Springs that allowed me to work around my kid's school schedule. Then something unexpected happened.

My daughter, who had moved out after high school into an apartment in Fullerton, and attended Junior college, was now living with her husband and our grandson, Jaydon, asked if we could accompany our first grandchild to a wedding, he was going to be a ringbearer in. I didn't know if Ed would be interested, but he agreed to take us. At the ceremony, Ed and I sat together. While I focused on Jayden, Ed paid attention to the preacher. Something the man said spoke to him. After asking around, he found the name of the pastor and his church. I attended another church, but Ed began attending the preacher's church, Freedom House, in Brea. The men of the church rallied around him and began including him in their weekly meetings and Bible studies. The men in that congregation reached out to him, encouraging him with scriptures they texted to him, inviting him to men's events, and such. All of a sudden, he found a new community. One radically different from his former friends.

When he came over to get the boys, I could tell God was working on him. He said he loved me one day, and I told him I wanted him to love God more. Then on another visit, he told me he had moved again. This time he had moved a couple of blocks away to a place on First Street, which was right around the corner from our house.

"Why'd you do that? I thought you lived at the beach?"

"Not anymore."

I thought it was weird, but Ed was drawing himself away from the beach crowd and everything that lifestyle included.

Our kids are now in high school, and on another visit, Ed told me he was available to pick the kids up from school. He told me about a ten-week course he was taking at church on discipleship. I was impressed. Then one day, he invited me to attend the Wednesday night Bible study at his church. I went a couple of times with him, and I could see that he was turning his life around. I remember feeling happy for him, genuinely happy. His presence in his sons' lives and participation at church were all bright spots in his life. But for me, this didn't mean we were going to get back together. It meant to me he wasn't lost any longer.

He asked me to begin attending church with him on Sundays. I didn't want to change churches, but when I discussed this with my sister and her husband, he gave some wise advice. He said, if we were going to work on our marriage, we needed to do it as a couple, so going to the same church was necessary. So, I made the transition, which wasn't easy for me. But after I had attended for three or four weeks, I was all in. I remember thinking, This is for me. I felt that God was speaking directly to me through the pastor.

What I learned is that healing and reconciliation happen in stages. And in the stage we were in, this church was helpful to both of us. Ed wanted to work on our marriage, and he proved over months that he was serious. He moved back into the house, and this time our relationship took on a new intensity. The real work began. I remember feeling insecure when he wasn't around. Was he out drinking? Did he have someone in his life besides me? Ed assured me none of that was the case. Still, I was dealing with trust on a new level. It took me time to forgive him for his betrayal. And I began to see the issues he was dealing with. Ed was angry, not at me, but at his life. I thought we were making significant progress, but Ed's demons and struggles had an unrelenting hold on him.

After an October festival at our church where I had volunteered to staff a booth, I arrived home to find Ed had left again. This was his mode of operation. He would just sneak out with his belongings when the kids and I were gone. It was so hurtful to us for him to come and go like this. I felt utterly abandoned.

I spoke to my pastor's wife, telling her that Ed had

left again, and I couldn't do this any longer. She prayed for me, then gave me a word of encouragement. She said they would be here for me. And I could endure in the God's strength. I remember coming home from church that Wednesday evening and thinking I needed someone to talk to. So, I called a friend, and she recommended a counselor who turned out to be a wise man.

John went into depth with me about why I was allowing this to go on in my life. He explored my relationship with my overbearing mother and how I had compensated in my life by wanting everything to be okay. I had allowed Ed to lie to me because I wanted him back at any cost. But if I wanted healing, I had to give up trying to control the situation. I could no longer live with resentment. I had to set boundaries for respect and honor in our relationship. John helped me work out a plan for when Ed came around again.

Ed did call, and said he wanted to work things out. Now I had a plan. Ed had never fully surrendered himself to Christ. He was trying to do the right thing in his own strength. I told him that's great. He didn't have the ability in himself to walk away from the evil influences in his life and repair our marriage. He needed the help and support of other godly men in his life. My conditions of working out our relationship was that he had to be accountable to someone each week, and it wouldn't be me. He had to find someone he could talk to every week or more. Then, he needed to attend church regularly, and it didn't matter to me which one he attended. Lastly, I asked him to get into counseling. Again, he could choose his own counselor.

He agreed to all the conditions, but I had no idea of if he would follow through with his commitments. All I could do was pray and trust the Lord that he would find peace in his turmoil and find his way back to a full commitment to Christ. I never gave up on Ed, but I realized I couldn't control the situation; I couldn't solve his problems. I could only pray and hope and trust and leave Ed in God's hands.

10

Our Marriage Restored

LINDA

In October, Ed left our home for what would be the last time. I wasn't certain he believed me or that he would ever return to our home. But, following John's, my counselor's advice, I was determined to stick to the plan we had worked out. He couldn't return unless he did the hard work necessary to deal with the issues blocking him from fully committing to the Lord and our relationship.

Within a short time, Ed called to tell me he had begun seeing a counselor. I had great peace and hope God was working in his life. It was freeing for me not to feel a need to be in control. I did not want to be involved in his counseling sessions, nor did I want to have a hand in choosing one. Years ago, before our first breakup, we attended church together, and we had three or four counseling sessions with our pastor. Ed became furious after the sessions, complaining that the pastor was taking my side.

So, I knew it wasn't a good idea to put myself in that position again. Ed had his deep-seated issues to work on, and the most severe of them didn't have anything to do with our relationship. Another counselor had told me that Ed was clinically depressed and had been for several years. Drinking had become his medication, a way of dealing with the darkness of his inner life. He was driven by needs I couldn't solve; he had to be willing to work out the solutions before God, to surrender his life, and stop filling it with habits that only covered up his pain. As much as I felt compassion for him and what he was going through, I couldn't live with his excuses and lifestyle any longer. He finally got that message and got serious about entering counseling.

I truly began to see that God was in control, not me. One unmistakable sign was the counselor Ed had chosen. Unknown to me, he had begun seeing the same counselor that I had been seeing. Thankfully, his sessions took place at a different location, so we never crossed paths in the waiting room. I convinced John it would not be good for Ed to know we were both receiving counseling from him. He needed to explore his own life, and I needed to do the same, apart from blaming each other.

Over the next three months, Ed would call and invite me to meet him for coffee somewhere, and we'd talk. He was impressed with his counselor and seemed to be making progress. But I still didn't say anything about seeing the same person.

One day Ed came over and asked if he could talk about what he had learned in his session. He said it was the craziest session he had ever experienced. "Crazy," as in it affected him deeply, spiritually, and emotionally.

ED

I didn't want to attend any more counseling sessions. My experience in the past with counselors had been poor to lacking. We accomplished nothing except to confirm that I was messed up. It takes two to tango in my book, and I didn't believe I carried the full load of dysfunctional behavior in our relationship. I had excellent reasons for the way I felt. But Linda had laid down the law—I had to go to counseling; I had to become accountable to someone. That was dangerous and scary territory, from my perspective.

Yeah, counseling wouldn't help this fool, but then what could it hurt. I wanted to find a way back home, but I had to admit that I was driven by needs that mastered me. I hated being dominated by impulses, but, hey, it was fun at the moment. But when I woke up in the morning, I felt someone had hammered my soul into oblivion. It was difficult when I didn't have work responsibilities, or I wasn't with my drinking buddies, to live with myself. This was an unexplainable experience to me, and I hadn't found any counselor who could fathom what I was going through, someone who gave me advice that made sense. I wanted my family back, but I didn't want to go through the counseling thing.

When I met with the man a friend at church had recommended, I do remember telling him a bit acidly, "My wife wants me to get counseling."

He didn't laugh, which I thought he would. Instead, he asked me about my problems, and I told him about Linda and our struggles over the last eleven years. I remember he stopped me cold.

"Who are you?" he asked.

A strange question. Every time I tried to answer it, he threw another question at me.

It didn't take the counselor long to drill down into the core of what troubled me.

Then the work began—on me. He refused to accept my excuses. Instead, he moved the focus of my thinking off Linda and began exploring my childhood. My teen years had been lonely, and I had resentments I'd buried. He kept digging at the roots of my personality and character—the deep reasons for the corrosive emotions behind my behavior began to surface in my thinking.

I remember leaving the first couple of sessions, my head spinning with insight as if I'd just had been dissected, all in a good way. I saw the raw edges of my true nature—I was angry—angry at myself, my mom, the loneliness I had experienced growing up, of a father who hadn't participated in my life and achievements. Most of all at the way I had messed up my relationship with Linda and my kids.

It was a revelation that Linda wasn't the problem. I used her as a way to justify my drinking and messing around. It took a while to take full responsibility for myself.

I had let so many habits control me—a spirit of addiction, pornography, lust, and anger. I had never explored why I was angry or allowed these habits to dominate my life. In my sessions, it became evident that they were a way out for me, an escape from my past, from my feelings of not being loved. Drinking had become an escape, a way out of having to deal with my misery. During one intense discovery session, I began explaining to him the history of drinking and alcoholism in my family, and he helped me understand the origins of the drinking habit that ran in my family, from generation to generation.

The counselor asked me to close my eyes. Then he instructed me to ask the Holy Spirit to show me when the alcoholism had started in my family. I did as he asked, closed my eyes, and began to pray. A starkly clear image came to me of a distant relative from Spain, a conquistador on a Spanish galleon on his way to the new world. Overcome with fear and loneliness, he had turned to alcohol and carried this habit into his life in the new world. My sixteenth-century Spanish ancestor had bequeathed to his entire line of children a destructive addiction that had destroyed so many lives. Despite the fact that I didn't have to succumb to the curse, I had allowed alcohol to become a stronghold in my life. When I opened myself up to the effects of drinking, I set myself up to become addicted. I let my addiction destroy my relationship with my wife and kids as it also slowly eroded my work performance. Eventually, it would kill me as it had some in my family before me.

It wasn't a farfetched imagination. I could not make up that memory. God had shown me the root of that sin in my life. Even though I hadn't started drinking until I was thirty-three, I had opened that door in my life, and the past flooded in, overwhelming me. I believed a lie that I wasn't cared for and respected at home. But my drinking buddies respected me, and drinking made me part of their club.

In therapy, I saw my addiction for what it was—an evil spirit that had manifested itself in the most destructive way possible. Yet, God was so merciful to show me what alcoholism in my life was doing.

The only way I could be free from my addiction was through God's grace and the strength of His Spirit. I could never do this alone. I had accomplished exactly nothing in my own power except to confuse my wife and alienate my children.

I remember telling Linda this story of the generational curse that I had allowed to overpower my life, and she was as stunned as I was. But now, I had a clear path to recovery.

LINDA

When he told me that story of the generational curse

and how he had repudiated it in therapy, I could sense the freedom he was beginning to feel. As the weeks progressed and we met at coffee shops and restaurants, I had a newfound peace that not only was God finally in control of his life but that our marriage would work. I just needed to hang in there and let God work. Every time we met, Ed had made more progress. I believed he was changing rapidly, taking responsibility for his actions. I could sense the peace in his life too. But it takes time to rebuild trust. On the way home, I often found myself wondering, Was he going back to his old ways? Was he hanging out at the bars and parties with his buddies?

He had lied to me so much in the past, telling me he was at work when in reality, he was hanging out, drinking. Or worse.

Forgiveness became an everyday event. It's not something that takes place once, and then you're done. Forgiving doesn't work that way because healing takes time. I wanted to trust him, and he was steadily proving I could. But it would destroy our relationship if I allowed the old memories to dominate my heart and mind. For my part, I knew Ed was in a battle for his true self, the man God wanted him to be, not the Ed who had given in to these generational curses that had driven him to a very dark place.

I prayed for him every day that he would win his battles. And I forgave him.

In prayer, during my day of errands and responsibilities, driving, shopping, whenever the sharp hurtful memories of the past twelve years, the hard words, the broken promises, the alienation of the kids, and the disloyalty in our marriage rose in my heart, I forgave him. I made a conscious decision as often as necessary until the healing took hold and the memories gradually faded. Then, as Ed took more and more significant steps in his recovery, I experienced the power of the Holy Spirit renewing my mind and heart, making me a new person, making me joyful to forgive.

Ed and I were sitting in a coffee shop in late December when he told me how much his counselor had changed his life. He wanted me to go and see the same guy. We didn't have to go together, but he wanted me to see him. Ed can get really insistent when he feels like he's onto something big, and John had helped him through a big life change—a remarkable life change.

A peace flooded my soul. The time was right. I told him I was seeing the same counselor he had been visiting the last three months.

He stared at me in shock, and then he smiled his big Ed grin. The Lord had orchestrated our counseling so we could each work on our issues. Healing and gaining wholeness in our individual lives was the only way we could heal as a couple. But, as wonderful as the changes we were each experiencing in our lives were, I told Ed he couldn't return to our home until the boys were okay with it.

For the last twelve years, the boys had grown up with a part-time father. For long periods, he had just disappeared from their lives. They were silently resentful. It wasn't like they were marching around the house, raging at their absent father. But they were not okay with his constant coming and going from the home. There could be no homecoming until they were okay with his return. I told Ed he had to sit down with them and hear them out, how they felt about his disappearing from their lives.

He did just that one afternoon. He listened in a sit-down with the boys, but I could tell he didn't like what they had to say. He had a lot of soul searching still to do. But, in time, he came around and realized that he had alienated them by his behavior and disloyalty. He understood that he had to work at repairing his relationship with them.

We had returned to attending church as a family, and while Ed wasn't yet living at home, he was just down the street in his apartment. He participated in the family, picking up the boys from school and activities and helping out more in the house. We had put off so many repairs during the years Ed supported two homes—his and ours. He never let any of the bills go unpaid, and the mortgage was always taken care of, and now Ed and I sat down and faced our situation together. I wanted him to know our condition, but I didn't want him to move home because it would save us money. I wanted him home when he was ready, when the boys were ready, and when God said - "Okay, he's good to go."

I didn't want an arrangement between us that was only good for the kids or our finances. That's not the marriage I wanted. I knew Ed never stopped loving me, but he was unable to live up to his words. There is so much more that goes into the word "love" that we often sling around so casually. It's an active verb that includes being cherished, honored, accepted. I had always respected Ed for the kind, empathetic, and hard-working man he was when we married. God gradually renewed my respect for him as I saw him battle and battle his dark side and win.

One afternoon, the four of us sat down at our dining room table. Ed apologized to the boys for his drinking and absence and promised he would make it up to them. He apologized that he had missed so much of their lives. He apologized for not being the man and father he should have been, that God wanted him to be. He said: "for the longest time in this house I didn't feel respected, and I was too good for this house and now I am not worthy to sit on that couch. But if you can find it in your heart to forgive me, I promise to make things right." It was a heartfelt conversation on all sides, and I could tell the boys were touched by his humility and honesty.

Was it time for him to return? I waited on God. I was convinced God's timing was perfect. Since I had renewed my spiritual life and allowed God to speak to me, I had peace in his leading. And now Ed's spiritual life had revived; I knew he was listening to God, and to his counselor. And he was hearing what I had to say. During our marriage, I didn't express an opinion when it came to crucial decisions, but now the dynamic of our marriage had changed. Our marriage was no longer all Ed and his decisions, but we were building mutual respect for our voices. When I told him he had to work on his relationship with the boys and hear them out—he did it. He didn't argue or moan. He knew it was the right step to take. When I told him I wasn't ready for him to come home, he was okay with it.

Each of us had changed in positive ways. We expressed opinions and listened to each other. We prayed together. We had been through so much, together and apart, that I knew we were on the verge of reconciliation that would last us the rest of our lives.

The day finally came when he moved back in. We were both ready. The boys were ready. It was a time of celebration, but there was still a lot of work ahead of us. It's not a walk in the park to come back together after so many years of separation and trauma. There were lingering issues that I had to deal with in my own heart.

When he left for work, thoughts of the past rose within me. Where is he really going? Is he hanging out with his buddies or working overtime?

Forgiveness is an everyday action. It's a conscious decision. And in time, it became easier to trust him, and he has proven trustworthy in every way. He has worked very hard to repair his relationship with the boys, making sure he carves out time to take them places, do things with them, and be present in their lives. He has worked hard to shore up our finances, taking care of needed repairs around the house. And we are both transparent in expressing our feelings about situations and decisions. There is a newfound intimacy in our lives that never existed before, a sharing of our deepest concerns and hurts. We both are honest with each other about our difficulties and challenges, our disappointments and problems. It is so liberating. We have both become the mature adults God wanted us to become all along.

I never forgot what kind of man I married, an honorable and stand-up guy. At the time, I thought he was perfect and could do no wrong, but that was a naïve and childish view of my husband. I was immature in my thinking. Everything is glossy and wonderful as newlyweds. The real world is that no man or woman is perfect or goes through a trouble-free life. I'm very thankful that I have become the woman God wanted, and Ed has become the man God wanted him to be, mature adult Christians.

We are both different people transformed by our journeys. It's been a long journey to wholeness that took over twelve tumultuous years. I nearly gave up on several occasions and was resigned to the inevitable. But my church family gave me strength to endure, and God led me to resources to help me in ways I could never imagine. As for Ed, he went through his own "valley of the shadow of death" experiences, and I almost lost the man I loved. Life often takes us over roads and down back streets and narrow lanes that seem like a foreign country, but in reality, if we're walking with God, we're traveling the byways of our souls and spirits on our way to our actual destination: a place of wholeness (Romans 8:28). There is a place, found in humility before God that He will speak truth to our lives, and if we respond in ways that are God-honoring, our futures are bright with His grace.

I've learned that if I stayed in God's will, in His path, I would pass through days of sorrow and anguish, but that is not the ultimate destination He had in mind for me. I had to cross many bridges, and I had to do it willingly—the bridge of willingness to explore my own family dysfunction that pushed Ed away from me, my willingness to forgive the way Jesus forgave me, and my desire for healing and wholeness.

Even though there were days I gave up hope of ever reconciling with Ed, God never gave up hope that I would learn the lessons I needed to learn. Instead, when I cried out to God for help, He heard my cry and was always faithful to give me the next step to take. And I think, if I leave you with one thought, no matter how difficult life seems, He only asks us to take one step of faith forward at a time, and He will guide our journey.

11
It Happened for Us

ED

We've been back together for a few years now but together doesn't mean perfect. We still struggle at times, but our disagreements have a completely different tone. Our way of solving problems, of communicating with each other, has changed because we've both been transformed by God's grace. I don't believe God inflicts pain. But the pain we both experienced was because of our choices, and ultimately our pain drove us to turn back to God. It took years for me, through many starts and stops, but God didn't give up on either one of us.

What's different now is that we both understand where we've come from, what we went through, and how we arrived at the place we are today—fully committed to walking and serving Jesus Christ. As a result, we both make better decisions in our relationship that honor one another and reflect Godly behavior.

The most significant difference is that I can detect when a thought is from the Lord or the enemy. Just because I feel justified in reacting to something Linda says doesn't mean it's right to. Now I know I need to nurture her in everything I say (even when she's wrong, though that doesn't happen often). As for her part, I sense a new sense of respect and honor. She goes to lengths to make sure I know she appreciates everything I do for the family.

LINDA

Yes, we communicate entirely differently now. We don't let things boil up between us until they explode. I remember, some months after Ed retired, and he needed to work again after his temporary assignment as a civilian employee with the Sheriff's Department ended, he found an excellent job with a community college district in Irvine.

Ed had retired from the Sheriff's Department, but he wanted to remain active, so he went to work as a campus police officer in an environment he enjoys, being around students and teachers. I didn't expect that this job would be as stressful as with the Sheriff's Department. Irvine is in an upscale part of Orange County, and he didn't have to deal every day with the criminal element he had previously. But after a few days into his training, he came home wound up as he had before. He was so quiet, brooding, I knew something wasn't right. I prayed about how I should approach him. I knew that I couldn't ignore him. Something was bothering him, and it had to be related to his job. Finally, one night, about the fourth or fifth day, we were in bed, and he said, "I need to talk to you about something. Maybe you can help me."

"Okay," I said, letting him talk.

ED

It was hard to speak up, but I knew I had to. Linda wasn't the problem, and I had no intention of taking it out on her, but my turmoil inside would hurt our relationship if I didn't get it out and deal with it.

My T.O. at the college, his name was Phil, "the guy rags on me, all day, like I'm a rookie, and I'm not. He won't even use my name, just says, 'Hey, Boot.' It's so demeaning."

He ignored the fact I had twenty-five years of law enforcement experience under my belt. It made me so angry that I wanted to walk away from him when he did that, but I knew that would be disrespectful.

"I need to talk to him, tell him how upset he makes me."

LINDA

He was pouring out his heart to me. It was a moment we had worked toward for so long now to be transparent with one another. As I listened, I heard God speak to me; He doesn't need your opinion. He needs MY words, not yours.

So, I listened to the still, small voice and gave Ed the nourishing words he needed.

"You're a man of honor, Ed. You don't deserve to be disrespected like that. So tomorrow, I'm going to fast and pray for you. Then, when you're talking to him, I'll be praying that you can tell him how you feel."

Ed agreed, and I sensed he had a peaceful rest.

The next morning, Ed let me know when he was talking to Phil, and I got on my knees and prayed for him that the Lord would give him wise words and a peaceful spirit.

When he came home that evening, walking in the door, he said,

"You won't believe what happened today."

I could hardly wait to hear.

"As soon as I began to tell him I didn't like the way he talked to me, he got defensive. 'You just can't take it,' he said. 'You have a thin skin.'"

"No, it is disrespectful."

That set him back, and I could see him thinking it over.

"Phil, I prayed for this job. But I don't need this job, and I don't appreciate how you disrespect me. I want you to know my wife and I are praying for you now that you hear what I have to say. You're being disrespectful of me. It demeans me."

Then he told me, "You know what, you're here for me, I apologize"

He went on to tell me that he was a Christian, but he had fallen away. He no longer attended church, read his Bible or prayed. Over the next few months, the man went through a real transformation, and the two of them became good friends. Phil has turned his life around and become a more effective officer and recently was promoted. Both Ed and Phil dropped their pride and because of that, they have become strong men for their families and God.

Ed had spoken into his heart and spirit and touched him with his honesty and sincerity, and now Ed and Phil call each other for advice and prayer.

Through this and other experiences, I've learned how important it is to set up boundaries that others can respect. This is the same process Ed learned through a lot of struggle and suffering. Boundaries allow others to honor and respect us. I see the same process with my boys that they honor me when they respect my boundaries. They are developing the emotional and spiritual intelligence to have their boundaries and goals.

Our healing individually and as a family has taken is still in process. It's a journey, every step of the way, along a path of change that is irreversible. We can never go back to what we were before. Every day, I pray that God gives me the words to nurture and edify my family and friends. There is seldom a week where I don't have some struggle, but God is faithful to give me the grace to learn and endure and become stronger in His Spirit.

ED

What's different is that we know now what's from God and what's not. I don't listen to the voice of the enemy anymore, at least I try not to. He never had my best interest and the interest of my family in mind. God does. Every day, I ask God to give me words that nurture and encourage those around me. So, I don't feel threatened by problems and challenges; God has an answer. He has the grace, the words of wisdom.

At this point in my life, I can look back, and I'm very thankful—about so many things. I think of my father, who did not have a formal education but was a wise man. He took the initiative to come to this great country and build a better life for me and my siblings. He and my mother made great sacrifices for us, and for that, I'm thankful. My parents appreciated what this country had to offer, and they became hard workers, good citizens, and raised responsible children. They were always ready to lend a helping hand to someone in need. They left that legacy of a giving spirit to me, and I'm living it now. A free man in so many ways, in a free country. I'm doing everything I can to instill in my children those values of personal responsibility, hard work, and living a committed life to the Lord.

I think of everything my wife and I have been through, and I have to say, Linda summed it very nicely when she told me one day,

"I don't think this happened to us. It happened for us."

We weren't victims of a careless spouse. We weren't casualties of an American marriage gone wrong. We didn't simply grow apart and go our ways. Instead, we are children of the living God under His all-wise chastening hand. He guided us patiently by the hand through the "shadow of the valley of death...." Up into the light of his goodness, to a new understanding of what it means to love and cherish one another, respect and honor each other, and care deeply for another human being the way He cares for us.

I think of that verse, "There is no greater love than to lay down one's life for one's friends." (John 15:13). Jesus died for us, made the greatest sacrifice for us—the cross didn't happen to him; it happened for us. He chose to die. It wasn't an accident. He died that we might live, and we live every day when we pick up our cross, deny ourselves, and follow him. (Matt 16:24-26) It's the greatest act of love. In a small way, that's what we do each day, for each other, Linda and I. Follow Jesus.

The End, but not the End.

Acknowledgment

I want to thank my Lord and Savior for being so merciful to me, His son. I thank Him for allowing me to be born in this great nation, with great parents and into a beautiful family. I thank my children (Nathan, Jacob, and Alejandra) for their forgiveness, blessing, and the honor of still being called dad. I am so grateful to have served as a deputy sheriff for Los Angeles County, I truly did live "the dream." To the men and women I served with, doing the Lord's work, you are some of the most courageous human beings on this planet. Only those of us who put our lives on the line for people who could care less for us, who hate us, and probably would wish us death, could understand the self-sacrificing oath that we took. Thank you, Randy Stover, for mentoring me as a young man and taking me on my first ride-along in the City of Lynwood, on a Friday night in 1986. My head is still spinning from all the U-turns and T-stops on Long Beach Boulevard. Thank you, Jim and Loraine Smotherman, for all your wise council. To Phil Romero, John Meyer, Jaqueline Zaragoza, Alice Griffin, John Del Grosso, and of course my pastor Josiah Silva, thank you for all your influence and support. John DeSimone, you were sent by God to help me in this endeavor, and I am so grateful that the Lord chose you to help me in this process. God bless you, my friend. Brian Hall, you are a true blessing, brother. And last but not least, "The Azteca Queen," if she were a president her name would be "Baberham Lincoln," my beautiful wife, Linda.

CPSIA information can be obtained
at www.ICGtesting.com
Printed in the USA
BVHW040154210422
634943BV00011B/266